Flying Saucers
Through
the Ages

PAUL THOMAS

Flying Saucers
Through
the Ages

TRANSLATED FROM THE FRENCH BY

GAVIN GIBBONS

NEVILLE SPEARMAN

Originally published as
Les Extraterrestres
by Librairie Plon, France, 1962
This first English edition, London, 1965

© *Paul Thomas, 1962, 1965*

Printed in Great Britain by
The Garden City Press Limited, Letchworth, Hertfordshire
for the publishers
Neville Spearman Ltd, 112 Whitfield Street, London, W.1

Contents

Translator's Note

THE READER may be surprised at the numerous references to 'notes' in the French Bibles. When writing this book, Mr Thomas made use of several French translations, the Little Bible, the Crampon Bible, and, most of all, the Jerusalem Bible. These versions are all officially accepted by the Roman Catholic church, but there are slight variations between them. Unlike the Bible with which we are familiar in Great Britain, French Bibles have copious notes at the foot of the page, in which the translators add their comments or interpretations of difficult passages. In the few cases where the French version has been radically different from the English version I have drawn attention to this in notes in the text.

In this book Mr Thomas has frequently replaced the word God with Yahveh, when quoting passages from the Bible. This I have retained when giving the English version. I have also retained the names Myriam and Joshoua where he uses them in place of Mary and Jesus.

In one case of a flying saucer sighting, it happens that I have personal reasons for believing the evidence to be false. I have given these reasons in a note in parentheses in the text.

Finally, Mr Thomas has given me permission to reveal his true identity—his works have been published in the United States under his real name. He is Mr Paul Misraki, the well-known French musician and composer of popular songs.

GAVIN GIBBONS
Shrewsbury
24 May 1965

7

CHAPTER ONE

There are Intelligent Beings on Other Worlds

SCARCELY THIRTY years ago, an important figure in the world of medicine, Professor Carl Jung, wishing to define the insolvable mystery of death, made this comparison: 'We are faced by a problem like that of knowing whether Mars is inhabited or not. And the Martians, if they exist, are completely indifferent whether we admit or deny their existence.' (Carl Jung, *Problèmes de l'Ame Moderne*, Correa, p. 240.)

Thus in 1930, the question of knowing whether intelligent life existed on other planets was given as the perfect example of something that could not be proved or disproved, a problem of the same order as that of the survival of the spirit. More than that, the question whether Martians existed or not did not seem a problem that would ever have any importance to us, doubtless owing to the vast distances which separated their worlds, Martians and Earthmen remained equally indifferent to each other. This was the view currently held until quite recently.

Since then events have radically altered that attitude.

The progress of astrophysics has enabled our scientists to conjecture that one star in six (others say one in four) probably possesses a system of planets similar to those which circle round the Sun, which means, at the very minimum, 300 million systems in our Galaxy alone.

As there is no reason to think that the Earth, among this great multitude, should be alone in giving birth to life, one feels bound to come to the same conclusion as M. Pierre Guérin, who said during a conference on 'The Plurality of Habited Planets and Rationalism':

'Modern astrophysics (not only) does not deny, but on the contrary, encourages the belief that Life is spread throughout the Universe.' (Cf. *Cahiers Rationalistes* no. 192, December 1960.) M. Pierre Guérin is in charge of the research at the Institute of Astrophysics in Paris.

Whether this 'life' takes the form of vegetable or animals, whether it is aquatic or whether it flies, is microscopic or gigantic, or whether it takes forms that we cannot imagine, we do not know yet. One school of thought among scientists, fearing a naïve anthropomorphism, thinks that the conditions on other planets would produce beings completely unlike any that we know. The other school of thought points out that matter is identical throughout the cosmos, and thinks that there are constant factors in the laws of universal evolution, which would ensure that life, on all the planets where it could develop, would evolve through similar stages. The possibility can thus be admitted of similarities between the forms of life on the different planets—even if these similarities are confined to similar structure—a chimpanzee and a sole, although so different in outward appearance, are alike in that both are vertebrates.

But the fundamental idea behind both views is the same; there is nothing to prevent the existence of intelligent life on planets other than our own. 'The speed of the evolution of species,' says M. Pierre Guérin, 'need not be exactly the same on every planet. From this fact it is possible that our mental development may well have been passed in numerous points in the Cosmos.'

This view is shared by the American astronomers Frank

10

Drake and William Waltmann of Green Banks Observatory (West Virginia), in charge of Project OZMA, well known among lovers of the latest developments in science; the project whose aim is to make contact by radio with the beings who probably inhabit the planets of the stars *Tau Ceti* and *Epsilon Eridani*, whose characteristics resemble those of our Sun. For this purpose powerful radio telescopes have been built and are aimed at the two stars. That it takes eleven years for such messages to reach us, and if indeed they succeeded in reaching us, we might not be able to decode them, does not discourage the researchers. As M. Pierre Guérin says 'it is not always necessary to hope for success when undertaking anything, after all, who knows if the first hertzian contact with other beings, of a mental level not very different from our own will not take place in the fairly near future? It is essential not to overlook such a possibility of contact, improbable though it seem to us in this year 1960, and to get ourselves ready for it mentally and to take stock of all its implications.'

Thus today scientists admit that life is not only possible, indeed very probable in other parts of the Cosmos.

The general public, which follows—if from a distance— the course of exploration beyond the Earth, is however, sufficiently interested in these investigations, for newspapers to consider it worth while to publish detailed opinions by leading personalities in the spheres of science and religion on the possible consequence of new discoveries in that sphere.

The *Figaro*, for example on 29 December 1960 asked R. P. Daniélou, Pastor Bosc, Rabbi Touati and Mr Boubekeur of the Mahometan Institute in Paris about the repercussions that might follow in their respective faiths if life on other planets was confirmed. None of these theologians felt that such a discovery would be incompatable with the tenets of the faiths they held.

On the contrary, the reply of R. P. Jean Daniélou, surprising as it seems at first, opens unexpected horizons, towards which we hasten to turn our attention.

'Does theology admit the existence of sentient beings outside humanity—certainly,' declared the priest. 'The teaching of the two Testaments and the tradition of the church *confirms* their existence. There is the example, for instance, of the angels, which we forget too often. . . .'

When his interlocutor, M. Henri Duquaire, showed great surprise that the priest considered the angels other than 'pure spirits', R. P. Daniélou 'burst out laughing' retorting that it was a matter of opinion.

We shall come back to this point and perhaps we shall have the chance to make our own interpretation of the reason for this strange burst of hilarity.

It is one thing to imagine that there is intelligent life in the beyond, but quite another to consider that a discovery of this nature could have a practical interest for us.

Here, the human outlook has developed as a result of the continuing exploits of our own astronauts. Every year, progress made in space exploration puts the achievements of the year before into the shade. It is now no longer a question of waiting passively for communications coming from another world; human beings will be capable in the near future of making a reconnaissance themselves of the Moon, Venus and Mars. In other words space no longer constitutes an impenetrable barrier for living beings.

Besides, if we accept the existence of beings of a higher order than ourselves, one is forced to assume that interplanetary travel, within reach of the men of tomorrow, has already been achieved by these beings and carried on in our time. A similar hypothesis, previously considered fantastic, now finds ardent supporters even among scientists. It is no longer rare in scientific publications to find the fact mentioned that life itself might have been introduced from another planet. This was the theory put forward at a recent congress at Los Angeles by the astronomer Thomas Gold; space craft had been able, he declared, to sow our globe with the germs of simple life about ten million years ago.

However, one could object that beings which had been able to navigate space craft ten million years ago—unless they were destroyed by some cataclysm—would have no reason to halt on their march of progress. It is only logical that these 'sowers of life' should be interested to see the development of their work. Their presence would thus have to leave visible traces on our planet and it is unbelievable that humanity, if it had really been visited by beings from outer space, would not have a clear memory of them.

But, in fact, is there no evidence which would allow us to speculate on the reality of such incursions?

An article appearing a little time ago in Russia in the *Literatournaya Gazeta* (9 February 1960. See also the issue of *Science et Avenir* for March 1960, the *Figaro* for 10 February 1960 and the international press of the period.) for a while caused universal amazement; according to the Soviet Professor Agrest, Sodom and Gomorrha had not been destroyed by 'fire from Heaven' as the Bible declared, but a nuclear explosion caused by extra-terrestrial invaders five thousand years ago. To support this statement, the Russian professor cited ancient texts, discovered in the grottos of Qumran, where the account of this devastation was accompanied by details similar to those caused by the explosion of an atomic bomb. It might be useful to compare this description with another text from the historian Philo of Alexandria and quoted by M. Daniel Rops in his *Histoire Sainte*: 'And when the flames had devoured everything which was on Earth they even penetrated the soil to sterilise it.'

On the subject of the possible presence of astronauts from outer space among our forebears, Professor Agrest cited also the terraces of Baalbek constructed of enormous blocks of stone (one of them is no less than sixty feet in length, and it would have taken about a thousand men to move it) which might have been used as launching platforms for interplanetary space ships. Of course, added the scientist, the presence of travellers from another world could alone supply the explanation of the mysterious knowledge of astronomy of, among others, the Chaldeans—Agrest did not mention the Incas in connection with this subject, as they were a somewhat later civilisation at a period when our ancestors did not possess instruments which were adequate. If they had nothing with which to explore the sky, it is obvious that their knowledge, which was so advanced, came from other than human sources.

It is worth remembering that other Russians have admitted anxiety about the immense explosion which took place in 1908 among the Siberian forests, devastating an area roughly equivalent to a small English county. It was believed at first to be caused by the fall of an aerolite of exceptional size. It will be remembered that the witnesses saw an onion-shaped cloud rise to the sky, a green-yellow light which lasted for twenty-four hours, the layout of tree-trunks lying on the soil in the form of a circle, the absence of a crater—indeed there is no evidence that a giant meteor had fallen there but rather that there had been an explosion of a large atomic charge at tree-top height. . . .

Perhaps in reality the explosion was caused by the head of a comet striking the Earth on its course as has been also suggested; but the point to note here is that scientists do not hesitate today to suggest publicly that there is a possibility of extra-terrestrial intervention, hypotheses which would have been received with ridicule a few years ago.

This is a fact which is most significant, and which should not escape our attention.

The idea that the Earth has, down the ages, received visitors of unknown origin is thus considered possible by the world of science today. But it is still a long way from these nebulous theories to the certainty required by our thirst for knowledge.

However if the evidence in favour of these visitations is more numerous than was thought at first, it becomes clear that our 'brothers from the beyond' not content to take an interest in Earthly affairs from afar, have actively intervened in them, of which the affair of Sodom and Gomorrha is only one in a thousand examples. It is essential therefore to alter our viewpoint. It is more than a right, it is a duty to do this.

Indeed, if the traces left by the visits of these space ships have appeared, up to now, so unusual and so negligible, it is because we had not shown enough interest in the research necessary in a sphere where there was little hard fact to work on. We had become so completely certain of our splendid solitude on this planet, we were sure that ancient legends were nonsense, and that space was empty, that the idea of discovering traces here and there of possible visitors from outer space made no impression on us at all.

But once our curiosity had been aroused in that direction, following the advances in astronautics as well as in astrophysics, the evidence for these invasions suddenly grows as if by magic. If this unusual research is pursued, the results will be such as to astonish us.

Lastly, if all these independent signs are linked, an impression of coherence is soon gained, and objections give way, one by one, to very creditable suppositions.

The documents which we shall refer to are all well known to the general public. However, we will satisfy ourselves for the moment with referring to them separately without trying to build up a complete picture. Isolated one from another, they do not—according to the plan we have in mind—teach any particular lesson. They circulate freely without exciting curiosity and many of them must be in the possession of our readers, who have copies in their own libraries without realising their message as they have not compared them with each other.

Who would try to read a letter that has been torn up without putting together the pieces?

Our analytical methods have scattered the elements of truth just like the pieces of a jigsaw puzzle. None of the pieces, considered on its own, has any significance; it is when they are joined together little by little the picture becomes clearer.

In the present instance the results obtained by joining together the scattered pieces is very surprising; they are so very different from conventional ideas that we have great difficulty in believing them ourselves. However, the fitting together of the pieces is so good that it is not accidental, the pieces of a jigsaw do not fit together unless they have been designed to do so. Such a collection of exact parallels, if it had been by chance would hardly have been believable and would deserve rejection as highly improbable.

It remains for us to observe with wonder the picture built up in this way and examine the facts that we learn from it, even if it means that we have to change completely all our preconceived ideas.

The result of collecting all this material does not merely prove the reality of our visitors from outer space and their intervention in the history of man. We are led inexorably to see the truth of another fact, no less strange: that these creatures—if they exist as we now feel bound to admit— do not remain secret and hidden from us. On the contrary they have made many signs of their presence, and if we still refuse to welcome the thought of them, we have to blame our attitude and not theirs. . . .

Certainly, such a statement hurts our deepest convictions; but our readers will hasten to realise that there remain certain facts, just celebrated and to which we will refer shortly, but which have received no reasonable explanation. It is clear that these 'wonders' repeated all down the ages and even in the twentieth century, are *signs* sent to warn us:

spectacular displays, sometimes taking place before thousands of terrestrial witnesses who see 'something' without
understanding what they see.

Such messages, unrecognised, misunderstood, were rapidly
numbered with the oddities of nature or attributed to collective hallucination and in the end forgotten about.

Our first plan is to run rapidly through the documents
which we have mentioned.

We are not expecting to find anything spectacular in our
first examples: it suffices to repeat that the isolated examination of each of the examples from our file will not bring
any unexpected revelation. It is the comparison of many of
these testimonies which arouses astonishment, and the outlook of our reader can only grow gradually when he is able
to examine all the evidence together.

A little patience is necessary when reading the pages that
come just after the end of this chapter and which give an
importance to theories which are quite foreign to the outlook of our day. For this reason we have reduced the number of these examples to a strict minimum so as not to dis-
tract attention from the main argument. However, if these
seem irrelevant referring to a distant past which is far from
the world of today, we think that they are destined to take
a foremost place in the thought of the man of tomorrow.

CHAPTER TWO

Angels

'EVERYTHING MATERIAL is ruled by the angels,' wrote Thomas Aquinas in the thirteenth century, 'not only the teaching of the holy fathers *but also that of all the philosophers*.'

By 'holy fathers' he meant his teachers in theology; and by 'philosophers' he meant intellectuals of all kinds, who had nothing to do with religious teaching; we would call them 'laity' today.

Thus there was a time when every man who had any learning at all took for granted the presence of beings from outside our earth in the midst of the life of our world. There is nothing surprising in the priests, who had to keep up a tradition, confirming the existence of angels, but it is much more surprising to find the 'philosophers' mentioned by Thomas Aquinas in agreement with theology on such a point. One cannot see on what basis these 'philosophers' based their thought, and even less admit that they knew of the reality of these beings by direct contact.

Furthermore, since earliest times, folklore has been crowded with myths implying the existence of entities little understood which one called angels and demons, gods, demigods, genii, jinns, trolls, ases, korrigans, goblins, sprites, leprechauns, marouts, adumbulus. . . . The names vary more, according to the country, than the character attributed to these beings, whose activities are often very similar.

Most people admit today that the belief in such beings, in those days an ordinary feature of everyday life, was due to ignorance and the naïvety of primitive minds; or yet a sort of fear of the unknown: man, terrified by his solitude, imagined protectors, companions, and even imaginary enemies.

But this supposition depends on one postulate, that is that it was certain that angels, genii, gnomes and similar beings did not exist. Therefore, the supposition concluded quite logically that they were invented by those who talked about them.

Therefore it must be proved that these creatures, or ones like them, do exist, so that the argument just mentioned loses its force. It is clear that if there were such beings, which are not on our Earth now, but which in former times visited our planet, the recollections of them all over the world, could, even though mixed with legend, have a certain bearing of truth in them.

It is doubtless too soon, at the stage we have reached now, to enlarge any more on this theme; the reader might risk being deterred by new ideas that are very difficult to believe.

Let us limit ourselves for the moment to removing a common misunderstanding which arises from the use of the word 'angel'. One can guess that this word does not really mean the conventional image which has been given to us by sacred paintings, making out the messengers of the Almighty to be young men with wings playing the lute or the trumpet. For many of us the idea of an angel has to conform to the idea in the Roman Catholic catechism—that is a 'pure spirit', completely without a material body.

But in actual fact the absolute spirituality of angels has never been declared as the dogma of the Roman Catholic church. A Catholic is therefore able to maintain, for example, that some at least of the entities included under the generic name of 'angels' can have a body without the risk of making a heretic statement. He can indeed, to justify his right to do this, give his references, the 'doctors' of the church such as St Gregory de Nyssa, St Bernard, St John of Damascus without mentioning Origen himself, who attributed a material form to the angels. 'The nature of God,' wrote St Bernard, 'is the only one that does not need the help of a body . . . but this assistance is necessary for all other created things.'

When Thomas Aquinas chose to take the view that angels were pure spirit, he based his views entirely on the works of an obscure monk of the fifth century A.D. who wrote under the name of Denys the Areopagite. But he himself was deliberately reacting against a tendency which was growing out of all proportion among his contemporaries. 'We must not,' he said 'be so impious as to believe, as the masses do, that heavenly and deified spirits are provided with a large number of feet and faces which they base on bovine stupidity or leonine ferocity and that they have been given the form of eagles with a curving beak or wings with rough plumage.' And he added 'neither must we imagine them as fiery wheels (discs) in the sky'.

These were the words of the man who inspired Thomas Aquinas, who was not afraid to declare in addition to this: 'It is perfectly legitimate to hide from the masses the holy and secret truth about the spirits of a higher order than man.'

Now we have brought to light the purposes of this holy man we can see without any doubt that he made no secret of his sympathy with the obscurantist methods of his time and his desire to hide the real truth from the majority of the people.

However, this ancient controversy about the nature of angels may seem absurd in a time like our own when there is no definite dividing line between matter and spirit. It is no longer possible, in the light of modern science, to draw

20

a definite dividing line between the two as the increase in our knowledge makes this barrier increasingly vague.

It is important to realise that in times gone by, the name of 'angel' was given to animals as well as to objects that were visible and could be touched. After all, what is an angel if not a 'messenger', if reference is made to the Greek origin of the word. Every 'messenger' from wherever he came, would, by virtue of that etymology, be taken for an *angelos*. The successors of Yuri Gagarin, Herman Titov or John Glenn, when they put their foot for the first time, however hesitantly, on the surface of some Martian desert, in front of a group of stupefied humanoids will be, in their own way, 'angels', messengers from Earth.

From this point of view, the traditional declaration, made in the second century of our era by the Christian philosopher Athenagoras, that 'the Creator has made and ordained the angels so they can look after the elements, the skies, the Universe and everything that is in them', corroborates in an unexpected manner the hypothesis made by the American astronomer Thomas Gold in January 1960 that life had been brought to the Earth by space ships.

CHAPTER THREE

Fiery Wheels in the Sky

'NEITHER MUST we imagine them as fiery wheels in the sky.'

We have purposely stressed this part of our quotation from Denys the Areopagite: it cannot help bringing to mind very recent memories.

The atmosphere of our Earth seems to have been traversed by discs like this all through the ages if we are to believe the evidence of the Bible, the writings of the Gnostics and also the sacred books of the Hindus. The *Mahabharate* and the *Ramayana* mention the existence of flying fortresses of metallic structure in the form of an egg or a globe on which the Asuras (a certain category of 'god') attacked the world. These craft, likened also to 'sky-blue clouds, brilliant as fire' were given the name of *vimana* by the Indians, and the prophet Ezekiel heard them called 'galgal' by the occupants themselves. (Ezekiel x. 13.) (See 'Translator's Note' at the beginning of this book. The verse in the Authorised Version of the English Bible runs, 'As for the wheels, it was cried unto them in my hearing, O wheel'.)

But these luminous discs were not always taken for celestial craft. At Rome, Pliny the Elder mentions somewhere in his writings the appearance of a shield of fire (*clipeus ardens*) crossing the sky during the consulate of L. Valerius

22

and C. Marcus. Gregory of Tours mentioned the flight of
mysterious globes of fire in 583; in Yorkshire a flat shining
silver disc flew over the monastery of Byland (Translator's
note: There are grave doubts on the genuineness of the
document giving the account of this. Two Oxford under-
graduates admitted to me in 1956 that they had forged this
document for a joke—but there is nothing to prove that
they really did so!) and in 1518 a 'star' appeared at the top
of the masts of the ship in which the *conquistador* Juan de
Grijalva was drawing near to the Yucatan, then this star
receded from the ship, giving off flames. It stopped above a
village and shot a luminous beam at the Earth. It remained
for three hours above this village and then disappeared.

A huge silvery craft flew over Marseilles on 1 August
1871, encircled the village of Bonham, Texas, three times in
1873 and appeared above Fort Scott, Kansas, the following
day. Several brilliant objects were seen above Kattenau,
Germany a little before dawn on 22 March 1880, while on 1
November 1885 numerous witnesses—among them an astronomer—saw a huge round craft above Adrianople in Turkey. The *Daily News* of 25 January 1878 appeared in the
town of Denison, Texas, with an account of the appearance
of a luminous disc; the witness who described it compared
its shape to that of a saucer.... In 1904, 1907, 1913....
But that is enough. We have taken this information from
the works specialising on sightings which we will mention
later.

Towards the middle of our twentieth century similar evidence began to come in from every quarter. From the end
of the Second World War unknown craft began to appear.
They were first taken to be the prototypes of secret weapons,
but their secret belonged to no one on Earth. During the
summer of 1952 the skies above the United States seemed
to be infested with them, thousands of citizens declared
that they had seen them and this led to many inquiries.
Then, after a short interval, a second wave of unidentified
objects broke over western Europe in September 1954,

many of them over France, the land of sceptics. In the beginning of April 1957 there was another wave of sightings spread over every continent, and lastly in June and July 1959 there was a spectacular display of them over New Zealand and New Guinea.

Since then occasional appearances have been observed here and there, but the press, discouraged by the similarity of the reports, gave up devoting space to news so commonplace that it no longer created any sensation at all.

It goes without saying that the majority of us refuse to believe that these mysterious craft ever existed at all and it is perhaps underestimating the figure to say that 999 persons in a thousand still think that these objects have only been seen by madmen, liars or drunkards, if they have not indeed been invented by idle journalists as they think was the origin of the Loch Ness monster.

The author of this book admits to sharing this quite understandable incredulity, until the day that the spirit moved him to do serious research on the subject.

He read several books of which some, which he will not mention by name, were obviously the result of a desire to produce something to sell, regardless of truth, so long as it was sensational.

Yet there were other books which seemed to him to be quite reliable and did not have the faults of the others. One of them is *The Report on UFO* (Doubleday, New York), by Edward J. Ruppelt, a captain in the American Air Force, who published the two year report which he had studied when at the head of Project Blue Book, an official body set up by the government of the United States to solve the mystery of Unidentified Flying Objects (UFOs). After he had systematically rejected the evidence of witnesses which was in any way doubtful Ruppelt retained only a small number of reports which he thought were quite genuine, and which he felt could only be explained by the entrance into our atmosphere of craft coming from beyond our world.

24

The criterion on which the official American reports were held to be genuine and which could not have any other 'natural' explanation were as follows: the object had to be observed and noted at the time of observation by:

(1) Witnesses on the ground.
(2) Pilots of military aircraft in flight.
(3) Radar.

It is satisfactory to note that the craft in question were not only observed by fallible witnesses, but were also seen on radar screens and could be measured by a theodolite, an instrument used in surveying, and which can be used for measuring zeniths and azimuths.

Thus when the sighting of a UFO conformed to the three conditions set out above, the report was put in a file marked 'UNEXPLAINED'—the incursion of interplanetary forces into our skies although admitted as his own personal view by Captain Ruppelt, was not made an official explanation.

The US Air Force has published several communiques, of which the most recent, published as the original version of this book was being written, on 7 February 1962, declared that 'nothing has been discovered up to now which proves that any one of the 7,369 Unidentified Flying Objects seen since 1947 has been a craft from outer space'.

It is as well to realise while on the subject, that the methods used by the American project to compile these statistics do not seem inspired with impartiality. Indeed, if for example, the description of a UFO could be fitted to a balloon, it was assumed to be a balloon even if after inquiry it was found that there was no balloon in the area at the time, 'for it must have been a balloon all the same'. In other words, this explanation is accepted at once even if it is not confirmed by any proof.

Despite this merciless pruning, the authorities had to admit that 1.94 per cent of the sightings between 1947 and 1962 cannot be explained. This figure of 1.94 per cent is given us as 'negligible', but a rapid calculation shows us that this small percentage corresponds to a total of 150 unexplained cases, or an average of ten per year. So an average of ten craft per year remain inexplicable and these over the territory of the United States alone. Is this total indeed negligible? (Translator's note: In 1964 NICAP, the American civilian research organisation, published *The UFO Evidence*, a large volume of 184 closely printed pages summing up all the UFO activity in America.)

As well as *Report on UFO*, the books of Donald Keyhoe, the journalist author of *Flying Saucers from Outer Space* (Hutchinson, London), show that they have been written in good faith even if they succumb occasionally to the temptation of his profession for sensation. This evidence is not confined to the facsimile of a certificate of authenticity bearing the seal of the Department of Defense, Office of Public Information, Washington, DC. A government department would not attach its seal to a work of fantasy. The evidence reported by Keyhoe gains a certain value from this, besides, one finds facts in his book confirming the reports of the author previously mentioned, Edward Ruppelt.

Finally, among French writers the works of Aimé Michel (*Lueurs sur les Soucoupes Volantes*, Edition Mame; and *Mysterieux Objets Célestes*, Edition Arthaud), show an unmistakable impartiality. The detailed reports that this author gives are partly based on the police reports from the places themselves directly after the incidents. When M. Aimé Michel is not quite certain of the facts he says so; when he is quite certain he gives his sources. His books have been translated into every language, including Japanese, he has correspondents in all parts of the world, and continues to collect patiently without looking for an immediate explanation, sightings of unidentified craft which are sent to him from every corner of the globe, including the USSR.

As it is not possible to doubt the honesty of many thousands

26

of observers who send in similar reports, among whom are doctors, astronomers, naval and air force officers, priests—it is natural to wonder how many are mistakes, optical illusions, and even collective hallucinations.

A book was written by the astrophysician Menzel which endeavoured to explain the sightings of the so-called flying saucers by possible confusion with meteors, balloon-sondes, the planet Venus and mirages due to a 'temperature inversion'. Unfortunately, the arguments put forward by Dr Menzel were notoriously unsound, for example when certain details given by the witnesses did not tally with his explanations, he left them out. Although full of refutation, the book does not prove that flying saucers do not exist.

There remains the possibility of a collective hallucination. But it is hardly probable that almost identical visions would have been seen haphazardly by men belonging to all social classes, all religious groups, all levels of intelligence and even—since the observation of luminous discs is not confined to the century in which we live but goes back to a fairly distant past—men of all ages and all civilisations. After all, those who declare that they have seen unusual objects are not usually found in the ranks of those who suffer from attacks of madness, whose evidence would be ignored by everyone. In the great majority of cases accepted as genuine, the witnesses were known up till then to be perfectly sane, balanced, of irreproachable morality and little inclined to practical jokes.

The psychologist Carl G. Jung of Zürich published a book entitled *Un mythe moderne* (Gallimard, 1961), which is a profound study of the flying saucer phenomenon. Anyone who reads the first half of this book gains the impression that Jung did not believe in the reality of these visions, which he used to illustrate a favourite thesis of the celebrated psychiatrist, that of the 'archtypes' which are always present in the collective subconscious mind of humanity.

According to Jung, the successor of Freud, and who

27

carried on his work, the human mind draws its ideas from a 'collective subconscious', the sum of the individual subconsciousness gathered during the course of time. In this way the endless repetition of certain dreams can be explained, which appear among people separated far from one another, as much by space as by time; in the same way this theory explains the amazing similarities in religious folklore among people, who, owing to lack of contact, would never have been able to exchange their myths. A certain number of symbolic images, always similar, make up the 'archtype' on which the phantasies of man are invariably based, even when perfectly healthy in mind. The fiery disc coming down from heaven, for example, can be found in all ages and in all places; it appeared even in the dreams of a client of Dr Jung at a time when the topic of flying saucers was not being talked about.

We freely admit that the whole theory of Dr Jung could give a fatal blow to the affair of the non-identified flying objects—if the probability of the reality of these mysterious craft had not been put forth ... by Dr Carl Jung himself!

In fact, in this same book, after he developed the psychological theory briefly touched on here, the professor begins a new chapter entitled 'Flying saucers outside the psychological point of view'. In this chapter he abruptly reverses his attitude and declares that after careful study of the file it is no longer possible 'in the light of human judgement' to doubt that the objects in question are indeed real, whatever they are. (Cf. *Un Mythe Moderne*, p. 254.)

He confirms what we said above concerning Menzel's work, namely that the astrophysician 'has not succeeded in explaining by rational means and of the evidence cited'. And he adds (page 249): 'According to the information which I have been able to gather we cannot deny the fact ... that flying saucers have been seen not only visually, but they have also appeared on radar screens and even, although much less often, on photographic plates.'

He asks then if it is possible that psychic projections could

28

give an echo on a radar screen, or if, conversely, the appearance of a concrete body on that screen could unloose beings
of a mythological nature (cf. p. 249); but he ends by suggesting—with every reservation—a third possibility:

'Flying saucers could be material objects, entities with
unknown characteristics, which come from sidereal space
and have probably been observed for a long time by the
inhabitants of the Earth. . . .' The increase of these craft
after the end of the Second World War, at a particularly
appropriate time in the mental development of humanity,
Professor Jung sees as a 'well-timed phenomenon', a 'most
sensible action'.

No one could express a point of view more in agreement
with our own.

It is, however, to Aimé Michel, that glory will come one
day for having discovered the first proof of the authenticity
of these sightings, thanks to this proof we can consider the
reality of this phenomenon as a certainty. We do not know
yet what this phenomenon actually is, but that it is something real is proved beyond all doubt.

When he was studying the details of the wave of sightings
in the autumn of 1954, M. Aimé Michel was brought to the
astounding conclusion that sightings occurring on the same
day were all situated on a series of straight lines.

It is sufficient to describe this by sticking pins into a map
of France to show the places mentioned in the press as being
the scene of a report of one of these unknown objects.
Towns, villages, stretches of road and other areas mentioned
in the press are stretched out along a series of straight lines
at times more than 600 miles apart with the accuracy of
three-quarters of a mile on a small-scale map. Let us take
as an example the day of 7 October 1954.

A line joining Cherbourg—where 'luminous globes' were
seen (*Paris-Presse* of 10 October 1954)—to Cassis, where
according to the *Provençal*, a very brilliant aluminium

object was seen—passes successively La Ferte-Mace, a point on the Route Nationale 138 situated between Saint-Jean d'Asse (*Aurore*, 9 October 1954) and Ballon in the Sarthe *département* (*France-Soir*, same date), then Lavenay (*France-Soir* again) and finally Montlevic, near La Châtre, Indre *département* (*Paris-Presse,* same date), all places where on that very day, 7 October, luminous discs, flying eggs, cigars, and even unknown objects resting on the ground were observed. That is to say, seven points along the same straight line joining the English Channel with the Mediterranean. But that is not all.

On that day the number of sightings sent to the press rose to twenty-eight; and all these twenty-eight points spread over French territory were also carefully ranged along straight lines; better still, most of the places in question were situated on the points of intersection of several of these

30

straight lines, making a sort of star-shaped pattern at the centre of which was Montlevic, crossed by five different straight lines.

There was a different set of alignments for every day of that extraordinary month of October, the record was reached on 2 October with its nineteen alignments of which eight passed through the village of Poncey-sur-l'Ignon, near Dijon. (The time when one passed from one set of alignments to the next was at one o'clock in the morning.)

The magazine *Science et Vie*, which, until that discovery, had systematically refused to have anything to do with vague rumours about flying saucers, then decided to break silence. Its issue for February 1958 published a complete account of the discoveries of Aimé Michel, accompanied by a map which in itself showed how important a matter it was.

Indeed the chance that this geometrical layout could have come fortuitously without any serious digressions, and renewed regularly every twenty-four hours, is, from all the evidence, practically impossible. On the other hand, after so much has been discovered, it is impossible that optical illusions, hallucinations, or hoaxes would have a tendency to occur in straight lines. . . .

The amazing discovery of M. Aimé Michel excludes any possibility of collective hallucination or coincidence. We must therefore admit that this phenomenon (whose nature and origin we are continuing to ignore), belongs to the domain of objective reality. The details of these sightings in straight lines are the subject of Aimé Michel's book, *Mysterieux Objets Célestes* (Edition Arthaud).

At this point the reader will ask this question: when so much accumulated evidence makes belief in saucers possible, how is it that the public is so badly informed that it remains convinced that the subject is nothing but a huge practical joke?

31

It is a fact that in our time a report is not necessarily believed by everyone even although it be true.

For more than ten years flying saucers have been the subject of discussion everywhere—people have talked about them all over the world. State organisations have been set up, not only in the United States, but also in Canada and Great Britain, to study the facts down to the smallest detail. All in vain; no 'natural' explanation was forthcoming, no certain proof, nor was there any valid proof that they did not exist.

People grew tired of them.

During that time books were written by authors claiming they had talked with extra-terrestrials who had appeared to them in a handsome human form and who carried words of peace and good-will. Young Venusians with long blonde hair supplied many exact details about the cities, the rivers and the forests situated on the other side of the Moon. (The Russians had not at that time given the lie to these assertions by their photographs.) Similar fantastic fables succeeded in throwing discredit on everything to do with the mysterious unidentified craft and anyone who declared his belief in them became a figure of fun. As the serious reports were mixed up with the jokes of the hoaxers, serious people began to refuse to have anything further to do with them.

So when Aimé Michel published his amazing discovery about the straight lines in 1958 it was too late, flying saucers had been judged and condemned. Although there was something new to add in proof of their reality, there was no question of raising the subject again: flying saucers did not exist and no one had ever seen them. There was nothing more to be said.

When Galileo published his discovery of the four satellites of Jupiter in *Siderius Nuncius* in 1610, the scholars of the day refused to accept his evidence; some of them even went as far as refusing to look through his telescope! They preferred to explain them as 'optical illusions'. Arthur Koestler recounts this episode in his book *Les Somnambules*

(Ed. Calmann-Lévy), and attributes their negative attitudes to real 'psychological purblindness' arising from the fear of the enormous changes in our outlook that would arise from such an expansion of the Universe. Koestler adds, 'This controversy concerning optical illusions, halos, reflections of light in clouds and worthless evidence reminds one of another controversy three hundreds years later; that about flying saucers. In that instance, too, emotion and prejudice allied themselves with technical problems to prevent a final conclusion being reached. Once again it was not considered unreasonable for scientists who had a position to keep up to refuse to accept photographic proof for fear of being ridiculed.'

Those who, nevertheless, have continued to believe and have publicly supported a discredited belief, are patiently waiting until a new turn in the events of history will justify their beliefs.

In what form do these mysterious craft appear?

Despite many variations and the inevitable inaccuracy of some witnesses, one can, *grosso modo*, divide these craft into three principal types: the disc, the jelly-fish and the cylinder, often called the cigar or the rocket.

The disc, flattened at its edges, is the type that most frequently appears and we may say, the classical form. It seems to have an extraordinary manoeuvrability, making movements possible which man-made craft are not yet able to do: enormous speeds, abrupt stops not preceded by any slowing-down, flying in tandem, right-angled, or even sharper turns, zig-zag flights, they can remain motionless in the air or rock gently in slow motion.

Technologists have suggested several explanations for these movements: according to their hypotheses these craft are able to create a force of anti-gravity around them, that is to say, they can cancel the effect of the pull of the Earth. Researches have been made to try to discover such forces

33

for ourselves as this knowledge would be of great assistance to the flight of our space craft in the future.

These craft have a metallic grey-silver colour like aluminium; or an amber yellow shading off into green. In certain conditions which we have not been able to define they appear in very bright colours, most often an orange-red, but which can change through all the colours of the rainbow. They seem to be turning rapidly like a wheel or a firework. They are equally capable of flying in zig-zag or like a falling leaf.

It is more difficult to give exact information about the jelly-fish craft; they take the form of a cupola or a bell. Round their lower surfaces a series of circular spots can be seen, which do not seem to be port-holes but openings for inexplicable protuberances, which stick out into space brightening the night with vivid colours like neon lights. It is these protuberances which have earned these craft the name of 'jelly-fish'. Much more rare than the discs, these jelly-fish seem reserved for a use which is beyond the limits of our understanding.

Lastly, the cylinders or rockets are quite different from the foregoing models as they seem to be flying bases—a sort of aerial mother-ship—which carry the discs for long distances. There are a number of instances of discs being seen coming from or leaving these bases. These cylinders are often surrounded by whirling clouds, perhaps resulting from condensation of the air around the ship, but which do not completely hide the rigid outlines of the craft.

On 23 July 1952 a silvery cylinder 'swallowed' two discs above Culver City, California. A cylinder accompanied by discs was seen above Denmark on 29 September the same year. The same thing occurred above Germany, Norway and Sweden.

On 16 October 1952 the inhabitants of Oloron in the *département* of Basses Pyrenées, including the Mayor and the masters at the local school saw a long cylinder in a cloudless sky at an angle of forty-five degrees giving off a trail of white smoke and small discs enveloped in smoke around it. The procession passed slowly and then disappeared, but a rain of gelatinous hairs like the hair of the Virgin—and later known as 'Angel's Hair'—fell on roofs, trees, and telegraph wires. . . .

Let us note carefully the description given by the inhabitants of Vernon in Eure *département* of a luminous cylinder, motionless in the night sky, in a vertical position, this, as we might point out in passing, excludes all resemblance to a balloon. It shone with a bright flashing light for half an hour, discs were coming out of it all this time. Another cylinder, in day time, entirely covered with cloud, flew against the direction of the wind above the heads of Vendéan peasants on 14 September 1954.

These descriptions are taken from the works of Aimé Michel already cited. Let us add this short paragraph discovered in the columns of the *Figaro*, 3 October 1958: 'Luminous phenomenon in the skies of the Pyrenees. The centre of scientific research of the Maritime Museum at Biarritz has announced that on Saturday evening an unusual luminous phenomenon was seen in the skies of the Basses-Pyrenées *département*. The object, which took the form of a motionless cigar of an intense red colour, was visible from several points in the district.'

CHAPTER FOUR

The Pillar of Cloud

'AN IMMENSE vertical cylinder, brightening the night with a flashing light and lighting up the surroundings; in the daytime a rocket of rigid aspect, surrounded by whirling clouds, moving slowly. . . .'

Does not this description awake the memory of a parallel in ancient times: who has not followed Biblical history as a child about the flight from Egypt and the crossing of the Red Sea? . . .

'Yahveh,' says the Bible, 'went before them by day in a pillar of cloud, to lead them the way; and by night in a pillar of fire, to give them light; to go by day and night' (to escape from pursuit by the Egyptians). 'He took not away the pillar of cloud by day, nor the pillar of fire by night, from before the people.' (Exodus xiii. 21 et seq.)

Thus, 1,250 years before the birth of Christ the heavenly guide appeared in this magnificent way to show the Hebrews the way to the Promised Land; in this way did the 'Angel of Yahveh' identify himself with Yahveh, or God Himself.

'And, the Angel of God, which went before the camp of Israel, removed and went behind them, and it came between the camp of the Egyptians and the camp of Israel. . . . And he put darkness between you and the Egyptians.' (Exodus xiv, 19–20, and Joshua xxiv, 7.)

36

We can just hear the reader's cry of protest, denoting, according to his temperament, unbelief or horror.

For some of our readers the wonders that occur in the Bible are little more than legends. There was no more a pillar of cloud leading the way out of Egypt as there was a vertical cigar at Vernon (Eure) or in the Vendée or in similar sightings by technicians in the United States Air Force or those in the Scientific Research Centre of the Maritime Museum at Biarritz.

For others the treasures of Holy Scripture make up a complete entity which cannot be touched and which they can only take literally if they do not want to run the risk of blasphemy.

But what blasphemy is there in all this?

If there is an author who could never be charged with lack of piety it is indeed M. Daniel-Rops, famous for his remarkable work on the Biblical era, so let us see what M. Daniel-Rops has to say about the episode in which we are interested.

He thinks that pillar of cloud, the visible sign of the Divine Presence in the eyes of the Hebrews, can really be explained in reality as nothing more than a side-effect of the sirocco of Arabia, the *qâdim*, raising opaque clouds of dust. . . . Is it less sacrilegious to reduce the Angel of Yahveh to a whirlwind of sand borne along by the wind than to identify it with a space craft, which carried mysterious messengers? . . .

Besides, we do not know how the author of *People of the Bible* explained the fact that this eddy of dust, which according to Scripture 'went before the people of the Hebrews for forty years', became a column of fire at night: what a marvel was this phenomenon! . . .

While on this subject, it is extraordinary to see that so many respectable interpreters of Scripture, whose good faith (and whose religion as well) could not be denied, so happily play into the hands of their rationalist opponents by attributing to a 'natural' cause, miracles which the Biblical

37

tradition expressly states as being 'the divine will'. Could it be that belief in the reality of these wonders would upset their preconceived ideas?

Thus the French edition of Holy Scripture known as the Jerusalem Bible, one of the best in the language (see Translator's note at the beginning of this book), is not afraid, in a note at the foot of the page, to reduce the 'fire from Heaven', which according to the prophets, fell on Sodom and Gomorrha, to a simple earthquake made possible by the volcanic nature of the soil. 'The text,' the note runs, 'allows the cataclysm [a seismic shock] to take place in the southern region of the Dead Sea. Indeed, the sinking of the bed of the southern part of the Dead Sea is recent in geological time and the area has remained very unstable until modern times.'

It is difficult to declare in a more questionable way that the prophets, despite their divine inspiration, were nothing more than mistaken simpletons, quite unable to distinguish between an ordinary earthquake and a fire sent intentionally from Heaven to wipe out two accursed cities. The 'nuclear' version of the Soviet Professor Agrest—although made by an author with a background opposed to religion—comes much nearer the traditional outlook, which understands the catastrophe to result from the intervention of some extraterrestrial force. After all it is the atheist materialists who, without wishing to, pay a tribute to the power of the Messengers of God.

Before we go any further, let us look at the treatment of the subject by those for whom the Bible is merely a collection of legends, and who think that this book today is no longer the unique document and is open to question; that it only gives a very vague idea of the history of the Jewish people through a mass of accounts that cannot be verified.

Excavations of increasing importance, the deciphering of cuniform inscriptions, the discovery of ancient manuscripts now permit us to confirm the facts reported in Holy Scripture fairly accurately both in space as well as in time.

Complete cities mentioned in Holy Writ, whose existence was only a matter of conjecture have been dug up during the past few years. Let us take Megiddo, for example, where the remains of successive civilisations were found on top of one another; in the level contemporary with King Solomon, stables were found which could hold up to 450 horses, built to plans similar to those of modern stables, and which the Bible mentions as having belonged to the monarch in question.

The accounts of battles fought by the Hebrews, recorded by the scribes of Palestine have been confirmed in a similar manner by the deciphering of texts made by the opposing sides. People who had been lost without trace, have sprung up from the past, their customs and their industries have been shown to be in agreement with the accounts given in the Bible.

Thus this book, for so long used only for strictly religious study, has been seen to have been changed more and more into a document of history whose value is no longer in doubt nowadays.

Cf. James B. Pritchard of Princeton University, *Archaeology and the Old Testament*, Werner Keller, *La Bible arrachée aux Sables* (Editions Le Livre Contemporain), and Charles Marston, *La Bible a dit Vrai* (Editions Plan).

Three months after their flight from Egypt the children of Israel reached the foot of Mount Horeb, better known by the name of Sinai.

Many years before, Moses, fleeing from the rage of the Egyptian princes had taken refuge in this same place, looking after the flocks of his father-in-law, Jethro. When his steps led him to 'the Mountain of God', 'the Angel of Yahveh' appeared unto him in a flame of fire in the midst of a bush . . . and behold the bush burned with fire and the bush was not consumed'. Thus runs the sacred text. Thus must have been the impression gained by Moses when he saw the iridescent reddy-orange light through the branches which is noticed sometimes in the flying machines from beyond: we shall find confirmation further on in this book of this daring theory which will lose little by little its illogical and pointless character.

Then said Moses, 'I will now turn aside and see this great sight, why the bush is not burnt' (Exodus iii, 3). But then he heard his name called, 'Moses, Moses' and he was forbidden to go any nearer.

After that interview it will be remembered that Moses returned to Egypt, provided with certain powers that are not usually found among men.

But it was not a simple flying saucer that led the Hebrews during their Exodus. It was, apparently a cylindrical mother-ship—something quite exceptional—the pillar of cloud which, with an absolutely appalling noise, touched the soil of the Earth on a natural platform situated some 6,000 feet above the level of the sea. Let us read once more the account of the incident:

'And it came to pass on the third day in the morning, that there were thunders and lightnings, and a thick cloud upon the Mount, and the voice of the trumpet exceeding loud; so that all the people that was in the camp trembled. And Moses brought forth the people out of the camp to meet with God, and they stood at the nether part of the Mount. And Mount Sinai was altogether on a smoke because Yahveh descended upon it in fire: and the smoke thereof ascended as the smoke of a furnace, and the whole Mount quaked greatly.' (Exodus xix, 16-18.)

Having been ready for this occurrence for a long time, Moses advanced towards the landing. First he received a warning not to allow the people to come with him as to

40

approach the craft would apparently be fatal to anyone who had not been immunised against its radiations. The prophet alone was able to come close to the craft without danger. 'And thou shall set bounds unto the people round about, saying, Take heed to yourselves that ye go not up into the Mount, or touch the border of it: whosoever toucheth the Mount shall be surely put to death: There shall not an hand touch it, but he shall surely be stoned, or shot through; whether it be beast or man it shall not live' (Exodus xix, 12–13).

A little later (it is sometimes difficult to assign a definite order to the Biblical events as the text is a mixture of various accounts based on different traditions, Yahvist, Elihist) when the danger from radio activity had lessened sufficiently, Moses was able to take Aaron and seventy elders with him, who were able to admire the pillar from a little nearer, though still at a respectful distance away:

'And they saw the God of Israel and there was under his feet as it were a paved work of sapphire stone, and as it were the body of heaven in its clearness.' (Exodus xxiv, 10. The translation 'pavement' is also found in the French Jerusalem Bible. Other versions have *ouvrage* (work).)

Instead of 'pavement' we would perhaps say today landing platform. On its scintillating stand, the vertical space craft surrounded in mist would be a frightening and at the same time a magnificent sight if it were anything like the rockets which we are accustomed to today.

After Moses was given the Tables with the Ten Commandments on them (we shall not concern ourselves with such well-known events), and the incident of the Golden Calf, which cost the life of three thousand people, the passengers in the space craft commanded Moses to construct a tent of generous dimensions with the aid of craftsmen from among his people: this structure, near the camp of the Hebrews, would be a 'Dwelling Place' for the celestial hosts. (Exodus

41

xxv, 8–9). This dwelling place would shelter the Ark of the Covenant, containing the Law and would serve as a meeting place where Moses and Aaron, the latter's son, and later Joshua the son of Nun, would come to get in touch with the visitors.

When it was built according to the detailed plans given in the Holy Book, this Tent of Reunion was a parallelepiped —a solid contained by parallelograms—of which the walls, on three sides, were made of frames of wood hung with purple or violet material; the fourth side, facing East, remained open, closed only by curtains. The whole thing was made rigid by metal joints. This metal had been collected from the children of Israel, bracelets, necklaces, chalices, statuettes, family souvenirs. Once it had been melted down it became bases, tenons, rings and handles: everything was of bronze, gold and silver. It was surrounded by hangings held up by poles of acacia wood, three hundred cubits long, which prevented the approach of the curious.

All these hangings had been carefully embroidered with figures representing Kherubim or Cherubs; we shall learn later, thanks to the prophet Ezekiel, several details about these visitors, who seem to cross space by flying machines like discs. We shall learn what they look like at the same time.

When everything had been prepared to receive it—the first day of the first month of the second year—the craft left the high summits to come down to the encampment.

'Then a cloud covered the tent of the congregation and the glory of Yahveh filled the tabernacle. And Moses was not able to enter into the tent of the congregation because the cloud remained thereon, and the glory of Yahveh filled the tabernacle.

'And on the day the tabernacle was reared up the cloud covered the tabernacle, namely the tent of the testimony; and at even there was upon the tabernacle as it were the appearance of fire until the morning.' (Read luminosity.) 'So it was alway: the cloud covered it by day, and the appearance of fire by night.

'And it came to pass, when Moses went out unto the tabernacle, that all the people rose up, and stood every man at his tent door, and looked after Moses, until he was gone into the tabernacle. And it came to pass, as Moses entered into the tabernacle, the cloudy pillar descended, and stood at the door of the tabernacle, and Yahveh talked with Moses. And all the people saw the cloudy pillar stand at the tabernacle door and all the people rose up and worshipped, every man in his tent door' (Exodus xl, 34–35, Numbers ix, 15–16, Exodus xxxiii, 8–10).

We do not think there is any need to add a commentary to these verses of the Bible; they tell the story clearly enough.

'And it came to pass on the twentieth day of the second month' (that is to say forty-eight days after the installation of the Dwelling Place), 'in the second year, that the cloud was taken up from off the tabernacle of the testimony. And the children of Israel took their journeys out of the wilderness of Sinai; and the cloud rested in the wilderness of Paran. And they first took their journey according to the commandment of Yahveh by the hand of Moses.'

Taken down by skilled workmen belonging to the families of Gershom and Merari, the Ark in pieces was in the centre of the caravan. When the Cloud showed its intention of stopping, the Hebrews made camp and the same specialists put the Ark together once more.

'And when the cloud tarried long upon the tabernacle for many days, the children of Israel kept the charge of Yahveh and journeyed not. And so it was, when the cloud abode from even until morning, and that the cloud was taken up in the morning, then they journeyed: whether it was by day or by night the cloud was taken up, they journeyed.' (Numbers, ch. 9 and 10.)

The luminous cloud, which the Hebrews also called 'the Glory of Yahveh', accompanied the people for a time in the direction of the Promised Land; then it ceased to be visible, although the presence of the people from outer space was still felt.

When Moses died, his powers were taken over by Joshua (who bore the same name as Christ, Yoshua).

Then there was a kind of pause, a period when, according to the Biblical phrase (I Samuel iii, 1) 'there was no open vision'.

The children of Israel had begun to doubt the truth of the tales they had heard from their ancestors and turned, for want of something better, to other gods which were honoured in the district. It was then that the infant Samuel heard once more the voice of Yahveh inside the sanctuary as if it came from the Ark of the Covenant, or more exactly, from a little above it. This took place in the year 1040 B.C.

But eighty years were to pass before the cloud reappeared in all its splendour: it consecrated the completion of the temple begun by Solomon in the fourth year of his reign, about 966 B.C., by coming down over Jerusalem.

'So that the priests could not stand to minister because of the Cloud for the glory of Yahveh had filled the house of Yahveh. Then spake Solomon, Yahveh said that he would dwell in the thick darkness. I have surely built thee an house to dwell in, a settled place for thee to abide in for ever' (I Kings viii, 11–13).

Alas! the cloud did not remain there always. A little before the fall and destruction of Jerusalem in 587, when the idolatrous Hebrews had put up statues of false gods even in the Temple, the cloud showed its disapproval by leaving the place.

'Then the glory of Yahveh departed from off the threshold of the house and stood over the cherubims. And the cherubims lifted up their wings, and mounted up from the earth in my sight and when they went out the wheels [discs] also were beside them, and every one stood at the door of the east gate of Yahveh's house, and the glory of the God of Israel was above them . . . Then did the cherubims lift up their wings and the wheels beside them, and the glory of the God of Israel was over them above. And the glory of Yahveh went up from the midst of the city, and stood upon the mountain which is on the east side of the city' (Ezekiel x, 18–19 and xi, 22–23).

And the glory of Yahveh did not appear in Palestine for another 587 years. It only returned to hover over the country to show, by its presence the universal importance of an event which seemed quite insignificant:

'And there were in the same country shepherds abiding in the field, keeping watch over their flocks by night. And lo, the angel of the Lord came upon them, and the glory of the Lord shone round about them: and they were sore afraid. And the angel said unto them, "Fear not: for, behold, I bring you good tidings of great joy. . . . And this shall be a sign unto you, ye shall find the babe wrapped in swaddling clothes, lying in a manger." And suddenly there was with the angel a multitude of the heavenly host praising God. . . .' (Luke ii, 8–10, 12–13).

Thirteen years later, a luminous craft, which shone in the sky like a star in the night sky, having mysteriously led the caravan of the Magi Kings, came to a halt—it remained motionless over the stable. . . .

But do not let us go too quickly. Although the 'Glory of Yahveh' was destined to play an important role in the life of Jesus several more times, it is probably better to delay a little in order to study certain facts told us in the Old Testament.

CHAPTER FIVE

Elijah, Pioneer of Petrol

DURING THE first half of the ninth century B.C. Ahab, King of Israel, married the daughter of Ethbaal, King of Sidon, whose name was Jezebel. He brought her to his capital, Samaria, and built for her a house which was inlaid with panels of ivory beautifully wrought by Phoenician workmen. (I Kings xxii, 39.) The city, surrounded by a semicircle of high mountains is itself situated on a mountain peak, from whence the view stretched all over the plain as far as the Mediterranean, was surrounded by walls ten cubits wide and had no fear of any enemy. Set in the midst of terraced gardens, the royal palace dominated the whole city. Its buildings were set around a shaded courtyard, where the Queen used to bathe in the fine waters of a fountain.

Whatever were the aims of the Cherubim in the land of Israel, their projects seemed in little danger at that time in any part of the Near East.

Towards the end of his life, Solomon wanted to please his seven hundred legitimate wives of princely rank, not counting his three hundred concubines from every part of the Earth—Solomon liked taking them from other countries. So he permitted freedom of religion, allowing anyone to worship his own God before the Temple of Jerusalem;

and from that time onwards the memory of Yahveh began to fade in the memory of his people.

The kingdom, divided against itself, had separated into two hostile nations, Israel and Judah. From Phoenicia—a country which is also known as Canaan—Jezebel had brought in an enthusiastic band of devotees of the son of the god El, the impetuous Baal and of his sister, the goddess Ashtaroth or Astarte; she converted her royal husband without much difficulty and the people soon turned to the beliefs of the King and Queen.

Trade in the mandrake, from its quality as a love-potion, prospered in every town in the kingdom. For Baal, the rain god, the fertilising water of the life-giving soil, expected from men an offering of their life-giving fluid. As a result of sexual pleasure being officially raised to the level of a religious practice, and the orgy to a moral institution, the priests and priestesses, or sacred prostitutes, were not sufficient in number, every woman, even the wife taken from her husband, was soon compelled to serve; she had at least once in her life—but it was not confined to this limit—to offer her body to the embraces of a stranger. But even here men became weary and competition began to take place. Simple fornication sank to something much worse and the temples and sacred places became vast brothels. Carrying their search of physical ecstasy to the most fantastic extremes, the worshippers, fortified by drugs, ended by slashing their flesh in the course of frenzied dances; thus eroticism finished with bloodshed, rattles, and cries. (Cf. Werner Keller, *La Bible Arrachée au Sables* (Edition Le Livre Contemporain) and Daniel-Rops *Histoire Sainte* (Arthème Payard.))

That was the cult of Baal for what it was worth and those were the temptations it offered to the children of Israel, the most chaste people in the world. It is easy to understand why the Yahvist Cherubim, who encouraged this chastity, took such a leading part in this affair.

At the time of Ahab, the Canaanite, competition had

hardly begun to win its first public successes, but soon it became very powerful. Only a few godly men were able to resist these lustful temptations and remained faithful to the law of Yahveh, which, as was well known, was strongly hostile to this type of practice.

Among these holy men there was one called Elias or Elijah, already well known for his exceptional ability as a spokesman of the Messengers of Yahveh: for that is the meaning of the word pro-phet, someone who speaks on behalf of someone else.

This Elijah was a strange man, a bitter opponent of all pomp and all luxury, he clothed himself in animals clothing to give an example to others; his general behaviour reminds us of the traditional picture of Christ's immediate predecessor, John the Baptist. For this reason, doubtless Jesus declared that there was a certain similarity between John and Elijah (Matthew xvii, 9–13).

Elijah spent his whole time proclaiming the cause of Yahveh, in the villages and on the roads. By his frequent contacts with the Messengers he possessed special knowledge which enabled him to tamper with the ordinary course of nature, either by taming natural power or by changing it. Just as with his disciple Elisha, and, much later, Jesus, Elijah was able to increase the amount of flour and bread from nothing, bring the dead to life and to walk on the water. (I Kings, xvii. 8–23, and II Kings iv. 1–37.) Let us quote here verses 42–44 of II Kings iv. which tells of an increase in the amount of bread exactly like a miracle of Jesus: 'And there came a man from Baal-shalisha and brought the man of God bread of the firstfruits, twenty loaves of barley, and full ears of corn in the husks thereof. And he said Give unto the people, that they may eat. And his servitor said, What, should I set this before an hundred men? he said again, Give the people, that they may eat: for thus saith Yahveh, They shall eat and shall leave thereof. So he set it before them, and they did eat, and left thereof, according to the word of Yahveh.' If the stories of certain travellers are true, certain initiates and Tibetan lamaseries have been able to do the same sort of thing.

The reputation of Elijah became great in his country and the effect of his preaching was felt even inside the royal palaces, where scruples had been put aside, not without considerable feelings of guilt. So much so that Ahab had a horror of Elijah and racked his brains for an excuse to kill him. Wherever his presence was reported, Ahab sent emissaries; but the man of God had always gone on ahead of them, and had disappeared without trace. People would learn with stupefaction that the prophet at that time was in another village, several days' march away; by such miracles Elijah became increasingly mysterious and more and more venerated by the people of Israel.

Unexpectedly a long period of drought ensued. This affected not only Israel and Judah, but Canaan as well. Baal had withdrawn himself and refused to send any rain. Jezebel's fishpond sadly displayed its rocky sides. The crops began to wither, the livestock to suffer. The King began to doubt Baal just as he had forgotten Yahveh earlier on, and the idea struck him to seek the friendship of the God of his fathers in order to obtain the water which the other God refused. He sent off emissaries to look for Elijah, but this time for the sake of conciliation: perhaps the powers of the prophet would succeed where the prayers to the brother of Astarte had failed.

Elijah knew the fate that would await him if he did not bring the rain clouds over Samaria. He had to ask for instructions from his secret protectors, for he would soon appear in the capital provided with several jars 'filled with water' as he said. But there was no water in that district. In actual fact these jars contained a special liquid, which was very inflammable, taken from an oily material. This material was found at that time in the soil when wells were dug, but only the few initiates knew its mysterious properties.

When he reached Samaria Elijah told his friends to conceal his precious load, and then made his way to the palace, followed by a wondering crowd. Ahab received him in his apartment and greeted him with a false cordiality (I Kings xviii. 17 et seq.)

'There you are at last, you troubler of Israel!'

And the man of God, clothed in animal skins, retorted, not in the least taken aback:

'The troubler is you, Sire, you and yours who have abandoned Yahveh in order to follow the Baals. And I swear by the Living Yahveh, whom I serve, that there will be no rain during these years except at my commandment.'

Ahab, ready to undertake anything in order to obtain water, crossed his arms:

'I am listening,' he said. 'Tell me what to do.'

Next morning the white, purple and yellow tunics of the crowd were to be seen on the side of Mount Carmel. Criers had assembled the people there at the order of the King. Elijah was to speak to them.

'How long,' he cried. 'How long will you halt between two opinions? If Yahveh be God, follow him: but if Baal, then follow him.'

But the crowd remained silent.

So Elijah proposed a trial of strength. He was alone, he alone was on the side of God; but there were 450 prophets of Baal.

'Let them therefore give us two bullocks; and let them choose one bullock for themselves, and cut it in pieces, and lay it on wood, and put no fire under: and I will dress the other bullock, and lay it on wood, and put no fire under: And call ye on the name of your gods, and I will call upon the name of Yahveh: and the God that answereth by fire, let him be God.'

Then there was a long murmur among the people and soon Elijah was acclaimed by everyone. Elijah had spoken, and it would be best to obey him to see on which side lay the Truth.

50

Elijah turned towards the priests of Baal and said:

'Choose you one bullock for yourselves and dress it first; for ye are many.'

And the 450 sacred prostitutes did what he had told them: the bull to be sacrificed was put on the pile of wood dedicated to Baal and incantations were begun, mixed with dances and bowing of the knee. The people, together with the royal family watched closely, looking out for the least spark of flame: but no fire arose.

'Cry aloud,' mocked Elijah, 'for he is a god; either he is talking, or he is pursuing, or he is on a journey, or peradventure he sleepeth, and must be awakened.'

Towards mid-day the priests began to stab themselves with poignards until blood flowed, but there came neither voice, roll of thunder or reply of any sort. Then the servants of Baal suddenly stopped and began to talk in groups.

Meanwhile Elijah and his companions put twelve stones on what remained of Yahveh's altar. They dug a trench all round it and filled this trench with the water in the jars that the prophet had brought with him. The dismembered bull was put on the wood and sprinkled in its turn.

The people thought. 'He has gone mad! He is invoking fire from heaven and starts by drowning the offering, and this at a time when water is more precious than gold! ...'

But the prophet had already started to invoke the name of Yahveh, and suddenly, as a result of the heat of the sun, the pile of wood burst into flames and continued until even the water in the surrounding trench was consumed.

The people had only one cry: Yahveh is God!

Elijah cried out: 'Seize the priests of Baal! Do not let any of them escape!'

And he drove them down the arid banks of the river Kishon where their throats were cut to the last man.

It is not for nothing that we have stated that the jars of Elijah contained not water, but a substitute for petrol.

That there are oil-wells in present-day Palestine had no influence on us when we made this statement. If the Zionists of today have decided to dig these wells on their territory it is due to their Biblical knowledge; the existence of the oil is confirmed in very clear terms in Holy Writ.

Let us read once more this passage from the Second Book of Maccabees: the action takes place four hundred years after the reign of Ahab and the story of Elijah, at the period when Nehemiah came back from captivity with the intention of rebuilding the city and the walls of Jerusalem as well as starting up again the cult of Yahveh, which had been abolished.

'When Nehemiah after he had built the temple, wished to offer a sacrifice he sent out to look for the sacred fire. For when our fathers were led into Persia the priests that were then devout took the fire of the altar privily and hid it in a hollow place of a pit without water, where they kept it sure, so that the place was unknown to all men. Now after many years [142] when it pleased God, Nehemiah, being sent from the king of Persia, did send of the posterity of the priests that had hid it to the fire but [on their return] they told us they found no fire but thick water. Then commanded he them to draw it up and to bring it; and when the sacrifices were laid on, Nehemiah commanded the priests to sprinkle the wood and the things laid upon with the water. When this was done and the time came that the sun shone, which afore was hid in the cloud, there was a great fire kindled, so that every man marvelled.

'... Now when the sacrifice was consumed, Nehemiah commanded the water that was left to be poured on the great stones. When this was done there was kindled a flame: but it was consumed by the light that shined from the altar.

'So when this matter was known, it was told the king of Persia, that in the place where the priests that were led away had hid the fire, there appeared water, and that Nehemiah had purified the sacrifices therewith. Then the king, inclosing the place, made it holy after he had tried the matter. . . .

And Nehemiah called this thing Naphthar, which is as much as to say, a cleansing: but many men call it Nephi,' (II Maccabees xix-xxii. 31–34, 36.) In a note in the French Jerusalem Bible it says 'This story combines the memory of the worship of fire among the Persians, and a certain knowledge of the properties of Naphtha, the local petrol, which was much admired by Greek and Roman naturalists and geologists.'

This name, from which our word naphtha is derived, is that of petrol in its raw state. In order for it to take on the appearance of water it would have to be distilled: and so that the prophets of Israel should know the secret of this relatively simple operation, they would have to be taught. Who could the teachers capable of giving instruction in a relatively advanced technique possibly be? . . .

But let us return to Elijah.

After the 450 priests of Baal had been executed, the most difficult thing to accomplish had yet to be done: to make it rain.

When it came to this, the personal powers of the prophet were not enough; he had to rely on his faith.

He sent Ahab back to his palace saying to him: 'Get thee up, eat, and drink; for there is the sound of abundance of rain.' But the sky was cloudless. . . .

While the king went back to his palace, still stunned by what he had seen, Elijah climbed to the summit of Carmel, sat down and bowed his face between his knees.

Technical trouble must have delayed his allies, for their contrivances were not in place at the fixed time. The anguish of Elijah was appalling when for a time he thought he had been betrayed. . . . But at the end of a wait, which must have seemed like a century, one of his companions jumped up, full of hope: 'Behold there arises a little cloud out of the sea, like a man's hand. . . .'

An hour later the city of Samaria was dripping under the

cascade of water which swirled away along the terraces and narrow streets. Elijah, his face turned towards heaven to drink his deliverance, made his way triumphantly to the ivory palace.

Standing in the doorway of her patio, Jezebel held out the palms of her hands to catch this liquid manna. She was laughing for joy.

But the smile disappeared from her face when she learned that this life-giving rain had been bought at the price of blood: all the priests of Baal murdered! It was too high a price to pay to fill up her fishpond. . . .

'So let the gods do to me, and more also, if I make not thy life as one of them by tomorrow about this time.'

So there was no chance of royal acknowledgement for the fertility given to the country, nor was there any hope of a return to the Yahvist faith. Elijah realised that there was nothing left for him to do but flee and resume his former wandering life. He hurried to Beersheba, which was outside Ahab's kingdom and left his companions there. Then he went into the desert and when the evening fell he sat down under a juniper tree. He wanted to die.

'It is enough; now, Oh Lord, take away my life; for I am not better than my fathers.'

But his hour had not yet come. He undertook, on foot, the pilgrimage to Sinai, forty days' march.

When he reached Horeb, he climbed up to a cave near the summit and there waited events. The night was still and calm.

'And behold Yahveh passed by, and a great and strong wind rent the mountains, and brake in pieces the rocks before Yahveh, but Yahveh was not in the wind: and after the wind an earthquake; but Yahveh was not in the earthquake: And after the earthquake a fire; but Yahveh was not in the fire: and after the fire a still small voice. . . .' (I Kings xi-xii.) The prophet well knew that none of the first

54

phenomena were a sign of the divine presence. But this tremendous uproar followed by a peaceful puff of wind brought a vivid memory to him—he remembered every word of the story of the companions of Moses, who described the first descent of the pillar of cloud in this very place and realised that he was going to witness from the inside of his cave the landing of the craft of the Cherubim. Then he hid his face by a fold of his mantle—dictated by prudence as well as respect—and went out from his shelter.

The terrible instructions he received contrasted strongly with the still small voice that gave them. At the end of the interview Elijah set out for Samaria.

The assistance of Elisha, an inspired labourer whom he met on the way, lessened the burden of the prophet to some degree. The two of them continued to lead the Yahvist supporters until the death of Ahab and under his successor Ahaziah.

When after the rather free use of flame-throwers (this is how we interpret the allusions to 'fire from heaven' mentioned in the first chapter of the Second Book of Kings: the 'fire from heaven' at the command of the prophet fell on his enemies and devoured them), when indeed Elijah had slain two captains of fifty and their fifty men, his position became almost impossible. Soon the news spread among the Yahvists in the region that the prophet was going to leave his friends.

Elijah left, accompanied by Elisha, whom he tried in vain to persuade that his new mission would be of short duration. But Elisha knew that the fate in store for his chief was that which until then had been enjoyed by one man only, called Enoch. He left the Earth one day to go to another place where death had no power; this happened before the Flood (cf. Genesis v. 24, Ecclesiasticus xliv. 16, Hebrews xi. 5). Elisha knew and he wanted to see. . . .

He did see.

Just at the appointed spot, on the other side of Jordan, a luminous craft, like a fiery chariot, appeared in the sky and descended rapidly until it came to the two men. Elijah was taken away from his farewells to Elisha, and the 'chariot of fire' began to rise rapidly in a diagonal which touched the tops of a group of palm trees. . . . Half drunk with fear Elisha remained rooted to the ground, calling Elijah with all the strength he had. But nothing was left of Elijah except his mantle, which had slipped off on to the ground. (Cf. II Kings, ii. 11–13.) 'And it came to pass, as they still went on, and talked, that, behold, there appeared a chariot of fire and horses of fire, and parted them asunder and Elijah went up *by a whirlwind* to heaven. Elisha saw it and he cried, My father, my father, the chariot of fire and the horsemen thereof. And he saw him no more: and he took hold of his own clothes and tore them in two pieces. He took up also the mantle of Elijah that fell from him, and went back, and stood by the bank of Jordan.'

At the time these verses were written the word 'chariot' was the only one that could be used to describe a fast vehicle, and the word 'fire' to denote a source of light. Farther on in this book we shall have the chance of telling of people at the time of the Great War of 1914-18 who used the expression 'an aeroplane of light' to describe a similar object.

'Whirlwind,' employed in like manner in other Biblical passages on similar occasions has the idea of a moving circular shape, exactly like 'wheel'.

CHAPTER SIX

Cherubim and Galgals

AT THE beginning of the sixth century B.C., in 598 B.C. to be exact, Nebuchadnezzar, King of Babylon, invaded Palestine, seized Jerusalem, pillaged the treasure of the temple of Yahveh and led the young King of Judah, Jehoiachin into captivity, and with him all his household, all the chief men of the city as well as all the workmen whose skill would be useful to him: potters, locksmiths, blacksmiths.

At the end of a long march the exiles reached Chaldea. They were treated relatively well and were left to organise their lives as best they could; however, most of them suffered from homesickness. 'By the rivers of Babylon, there we sat down, yea, we wept when we remembered Zion. We hanged our harps upon the willows in the midst thereof. For there they that carried us away captive required of us a song: and they that wasted us required of us mirth, saying, Sing us one of the songs of Zion. How shall We sing Yahveh's song in a strange land?' (Psalm cxxxvii, 1–4.)

But it was indeed 'by the river of Babylon', the Khobar, that Ezekiel was sitting sadly, 'the fifth day of the fourth month of the fifth year since the first captivity'—that is to say in the year 593 B.C., when he saw the 'chariot of Yahveh' appear in the sky above his head.

The Biblical account of the 'vision' of Ezekiel is notable for its extraordinary obscurity. Up to now Biblical commentators, not trying to interpret it in a literal sense, have taken the view that it consists of nothing more than a series of symbols whose meaning has been lost in the mists of time. The prophet, they declare, makes use of a literary device which was very much in vogue in his day—apocalyptic writing. He aimed to proclaim fundamental truths by concealing them in poetic imagery, whose austere secrets left the user of them out of breath.

It is clear that we cannot share this view.

Let us note first the precision with which our 'visionary' tells us the exact date of the happenings he is preparing to tell us about: 'the fifth day of the fourth month of the fifth year. . . .' This event does not take place at some vague time in the past but that very day. Such attention to detail is unusual in Biblical annals and this piece of information is evidence in favour of the accuracy of the evidence.

'And I looked,' he tells us in Ezekiel i. 4, 'and behold a whirlwind came out of the north, a great cloud, and a fire infolding itself, and a brightness was about it, and out of the midsts thereof as the colour of amber, out of the midsts of the fire. Now (Ezekiel i. 15) as I beheld the living creatures behold one wheel upon the earth by the living creatures, with his four faces. The appearance of the wheels and their work was like unto the colour of a beryl;' [A greenish sheen, but light yellow in colour: these are expressions that occur over and over again in modern reports of unidentified flying objects] 'and they four had one likeness: and their appearance and their work was as it were a wheel in the middle of a wheel. When they went, they went upon their four sides, and they turned not when they went' [Other texts give 'they do not turn round when they move'—a statement that is meaningless in reference to 'wheels'.] 'As for their rings, they were so high that they were dreadful; and their rings were full of eyes round about them four.' [Here the French Jerusalem Bible has a note 'Text obscure and translation uncertain'. Some writers, assuming as we do that this might be a description of a space craft thought these 'eyes' were portholes round the craft. But modern reports of flying saucers hardly ever mention such portholes; however we have seen that the 'jelly-fish', just as round in shape, have a series of such openings all round their circumference, occasionally used so they can extend their enigmatic legs. Perhaps the 'wheels' of Ezekiel were really this type of craft.]

'And when the living creatures went, the wheels went by them: and when the living creatures were lifted up from the earth, the wheels were lifted up. Whithersoever the spirit was to go, they went, thither was their spirit to go; and the wheels were lifted up over against them: for the spirit of the living creature was in the wheels.'

But the vision by the river Khobar was not limited to that particular aspect: above the discs the 'mother ship' was floating—'Something,' as Ezekiel said, 'that had the appearance of the likeness of the glory of Yahveh.'

The Glory of Yahveh: we have seen this description given in earlier books to the pillars of cloud and fire. It is difficult to understand the difficulty which faced the man of the sixth century B.C. who was trying to express by means of the language of his time a vision of something that was quite outside his knowledge; a difficulty which the scribes would share when they tried to write down, from memory, the words of their master.

For, if one is to believe the commentator in the French Jerusalem Bible in his chapter on the prophets, it is unlikely that the book of Ezekiel was written by the prophet himself in one attempt, the contradictions and clumsy passages it contains make one think of the work of 'disciples working on other writings, or memories, combining them and putting the finishing touches to them'.

Where there are two descriptions following one another in the text (the first in chapter 1, 26 et seq., the second in chapter 8, 2 et seq.) there are notable variations when one is compared with the other. This is what stands out:

Above the four animals and their discs (wheels) there was

'a sort of throne in sapphire stone', and above the throne, high up, a luminous form (and not 'a being of human appearance' as the Greek version states, when the Hebrew original speaks of a 'being of fire). In the upper part of the craft ('behind what appeared to be his loins and above') one could make out a metallic lustre, when the lower part ('behind what appeared to be his loins and below') disappeared in a jet of flames projecting all round in colours 'similar to the rainbow which appears in the clouds on rainy days'.

Terrified, Ezekiel fell on his face to the ground. Here, let us pay careful attention: the 'thing' then stretched in the direction of the prophet 'a sort of hand' which seized him. There he was, taken up from the ground, suspended between the earth and heaven, and transported 'in divine visions' the whole distance between Babylon and Jerusalem, some 500 miles as the crow flies. He found himself, more dead than alive, in the square in front of the Temple, exactly at the entrance of the interior porch on the north side. In front of him he recognised the glory of Yahveh, the Cherubim with all their finery, plus a man clothed in white linen. . . .

Let us look again at the verses which describe the four 'living beings' or 'animals', that is to say, our extra-terrestrials, and regroup them. It is not without reason that we are putting the patience of our readers to the test, all the details that follow, even though they may seem unimportant to the reader, have really a great importance in the unbelievable facts they bring together as will be shown in the following chapter.

Ezekiel begins by saying that these 'beings' have human form, but it can soon be seen that this similarity to man does not go very far. Without a doubt the 'living creatures' in question bore a certain resemblance to us in the sense that they appeared to stand in a vertical position and possessed a head, a body and legs.

But 'their feet were straight feet and the sole of their feet was like the sole of a calf's foot': exactly like the satyrs of Attica. Ezekiel tells us they had wings, four in number, two of which were raised vertically above them; the two others were covering their bodies; but as the presence of these wings, also mentioned by Isiah, is the only characteristic that does not tally with our non-Biblical notions which we possess on the subject of these entities, we are led to believe that they were either added for expediency (a flying entity would be bound to have wings) or that they were some sort of technical apparatus and the prophet mistook them for wings.

'Human hands appeared under these wings'—but not arms.

'And the likeness of the firmament upon the heads of the living creature was as the colour of terrible crystal, stretched forth over their heads above. . . .' This would correspond to the wearing of a translucent space-suit.

There remain several verses hard to understand which seem to have given a lot of trouble to the translators. All through the chapter in the French Jerusalem Bible there are notes and cross-references like this: 'Translation is doubtful'—'certain details of the vision are obscure'—'Unintelligible Hebrew'.

The passage in question is well known:

'And every one had four faces and every one had four wings. . . . As for the likeness of their faces, they four had the face of a man, and the face of a lion, on the right side: and they four had the face of an ox on the left side; they four had also the face of an eagle.'

One cannot help wondering how it is possible to march 'straight ahead' when one had four faces turned to the four points of the compass: but fortunately for us verse 14 of chapter 10 enables us to obtain a more coherent and less startling description:

'And every one had four faces: the first face was the face of a cherub, and the second face was the face of a

61

man, and the third the face of a lion, and the fourth the face of an eagle.'

This passage gives us an important detail concerning the true nature of the Cherubim: of the four living creatures, only one really had the face of a Cherub proper, and not the one with the face of a lion, nor the one with the face of an eagle, nor even the one with the face of a man. It is therefore the one who resembled a bull—and we have also seen that he borrowed the hoof from this animal also.

Is it necessary at this stage to confute the objection which will certainly be made? The poetic character of the book of Ezekiel will be put forward as an objection. This four-fold man-eagle-bull-lion, which is mentioned later on by St John in the Revelation, was identified in Christian times by St Ireneus as the four evangelists, Luke, John, Matthew and Mark respectively?

In our mind there is no doubt at all that this curious collection has no symbolic significance at all, especially as the experts on the subject do not agree among themselves as to what meaning should be given to them.

For our part we think that the four faces turned to the four points of the compass could allude to the signs of the zodiac, two of which are mentioned explicity: the lion and the bull. On the other hand it is well known that the eagle, who according to the Greeks carried off Ganymede and made him the cup-bearer of the Gods, the water-carrier, is one of the attributes of the sign which bears the name (Water-carrier or Aquarius). To form the cross, there remains the scorpion, which, in the view of certain authors is the sign of man.

In any case, whatever be the meaning of the message which was given to Ezekiel to pass on to us, and which he did not know how—or did not wish—to make clear to us, the main thing is that there was clearly the intention to give a message.

62

Let us, at this point, consider the origin of the word 'Cherub'.

'I knew then,' said Ezekiel, 'that [these beings] were Cherubim [plural of Cherub] . . . I heard that they gave their discs the name of "galgal".'

The use of the word 'galgal' comes again in Joshua iv. 19, when it describes a monument commemorating Divine intervention; it consisted of a heap of stones circular in shape—which will no longer be a surprise to us—and which gives its name to the town of Galgala. (In other versions of the French Bible 'galgal' is translated as 'nimble' (Crampon). Other 'galgals' are found in Brittany, consisting of piles of stones on top of tombstones, (from Breton, gal = pebble).

But what about the Cherubim?

Linguistic authorities tell us that this word originates in Chaldea, where the Kirubi and Karibu were the names given to flying genii belonging at the same time to the bull, the lion, the man, and the eagle. The famous winged bulls that can be seen by visitors to the Louvre in Paris are of Kirubi. Statues of these Kirubi, carved in the brickwork, surrounded the doors of houses in Babylon, to protect the inhabitants from evil spirits. As Ezekiel had been carried away to Chaldea at the time he had this wonderful meeting, he described the beings he met in the terms in current use in Babylon. The Hebrew language borrowed the word and changed it to Cherub and it was used to give a name to a certain type of messenger from on high, as was the word Seraph, in the plural Seraphim.

But these Kirubi or Karibu did not confine their appearances to the Middle East. Their name and some of their qualities are similar to those of beings which the Greeks dreaded to meet on the borders of their forests and which they called the Korybantes. The Greeks said that they had come down from the Sun, a phrase which has a very special meaning for us and fits in with what we know of the Cherubim, who also came down in a shining disc from time to time.... The Persians had a cult of the Sun, which they called Khor. On the other hand, the Bretons, who use the word 'galgal', tell stories of beings called Korrigans.

But it does not stop there, for in the sub-polar regions the Eskimo declare that they have met Caribous which have little similarity to reindeer, but seem to be a mixture of deer and man. It is impossible to bring these caribou down with rifle bullets.

Finally, there is a race which lives in the Antilles whose origin is unknown; they are short, with wide shoulders, thickset, but having slender limbs. They are the Karib, and their name has been distorted to Caraïbes. There is a possibility that the name was given them from a resemblance which we shall come back to later.

For the passengers in the discs have not limited their personal contacts with men on Earth to ancient times: they have appeared in every age, even to the present time; to several men on Earth, who would consider themselves lucky to have this privilege.

CHAPTER SEVEN

Little Men Cause Great Terror

WOULD THERE be anything extraordinary if, after adventures like this the Prophet Ezekiel spent some time in thinking about similar adventures? After his experience at the river Khobar he lost the power of speech and remained 'for seven days stupefied among his friends'.

At the present time our evolution in the scientific and technical fields makes us take for granted things that would have been the cause of fear and wonder to our ancestors—imagine Ezekiel, Socrates or Vercingetorix in the presence of a locomotive at speed, a blast furnace, a helicopter or a jet aircraft. Yet in spite of this we do not like it when we accidentally see a phenomenon which we cannot explain at once from the knowledge we possess.

This was the case when a metal-worker on the Franco-Belgian frontier near Valenciennes heard dogs barking at 22.30 on Friday, 10 September 1954. He went out of his house and saw a dark mass some twenty feet from his door. Then, hearing the sound of running feet, he shone his electric torch in that direction and saw in the beam of light two 'beings' who were walking along behind a palisade; one of them turned back for a moment in the direction of the light, and the place where his face should have been gave off a reflection which might have been of glass or of metal. They were both very short in height but had very wide shoulders,

65

with small legs—just like the Karib in the Antilles. They did not seem to have any arms.

Thinking that they were smugglers, the metal worker dashed to the garden gate to cut off the two fugitives: he was only about six feet from them when a light as brilliant as that given off by magnesium forced him to close his eyes. He tried to cry out, but was unable to; and to move, but his muscles would not work. When the light went out and he regained control of his muscles, he saw the dark mass, which he had already seen when he came out of his house, rise vertically like a helicopter; a thick vapour gushed out underneath with a light hissing sound. The craft rose up, then became red in colour and went away towards the west.

The metal-worker, slowly regaining courage, rushed to the nearest police station; but he was so worked up that they thought he was drunk. He then went to the commissariat of police. Trembling in every limb, he was unable to make a statement, for he was suffering from severe stomach pains. The commissioner of police soon rejected the theory that it was a practical joke, as the fear of the man was too obvious. . . .

The enquiry, carried out jointly by the civil police, and the air police found on the spot shown to them, markings suggesting a weight of nearly thirty tons, stones with heat marks on them and several blackened spots. But there were no traces of footsteps. . . . It is true that they expected to find prints of human feet.

This account, like the ones that follow, are described in the book by Aimé Michel: *Mysterieux Objets Célestes* (Editions Arthaud). Aimé Michel, who received permission to record the official reports, tells the story of M. Dewilde, the metal-worker who was the hero of this adventure, and notes that five other persons saw the object. They lived in nearby villages and, at the same time, saw a red light moving in the sky, seeming to come from Quarouble, where M. Dewilde lived. This certainly seems to corroborate this amazing story.

The same source gives the following story: On 26 September 1954 in a village a few miles east of Valence about 14.30 a woman was peacefully picking mulberries when her little dog began to howl its head off. Looking in the direction of a field of maize, she thought she could see a fan-shaped object about three feet high. It consisted of a diving suit of translucent plastic with a globe on the top. Intrigued, she went up to it and could make out inside the suit something which was looking at her with three large eyes. At that moment the fan-shaped object began to walk towards the lady, waddling lightly, but at a very fast pace. The lady let out a cry, took to her heels and hid herself in a little wood. Then all the dogs in the village began to bark. A few minutes later an object fairly large in size rose up from behind a clump of trees and made off, brushing the maize shoots with a kind of hissing noise; it gained height and disappeared to the north-east.

All the noises that the craft had made had been heard by the neighbours. In the place by the clump of trees where the craft had taken off there was a circle of bushes and shrubs which had been crushed, several feet of the surrounding maize was lying down in lines radiating from where the craft had landed.

The lady had to go to bed, the victim of a severe fever. The report of the local police said that the fright had brought on certain troubles which are confined to women. The little dog remained trembling with fright for three days.

(There is nothing to make us take this story seriously if the event in question—it took place at Chabeuil in the *département* of Drome—did not illustrate the 'straight line theory' which M. Aimé Michel puts forth. Indeed that very same day an 'unknown object aluminium in colour' was seen by a former artillery observer above Challes-les-Eaux (Savoie), whilst the passengers in a bus and a group of roadmen noticed a reddish luminous object, first in the sky, then down in a field near Foussignargues (Gard). A straight line drawn from Foussignargues to Challes-les-Eaux passes through Chabeuil.)

Several days earlier, on 17 September 1954 at 22.30 a 'little man' appeared to a cyclist who had had a strange sensation of paralysis and who as a result had been forced to stop at the side of the road several miles from Clermont Ferrand. A dark mass, giving off a green light hurriedly rose up from the ground and then disappeared in the sky at an astounding speed. The cyclist took the road again, trembling with fear.

(The same comment applies here as above: one would be tempted to dismiss the story if the appearances of unknown objects had not taken place the same day not only near Clermont-Ferrand, but also at Chatellerault (Vienne), at Chaudolas (Ardèche) and at Rome in Italy—all places which are situated on the same straight line. Thus, observes Aimé Michel, there are four people or groups of people with strange stories who are exactly in a straight line between Rome and Chatellerault in the same twenty-four hours. Is it incredible?

Lastly on Saturday 9 October 1954 about 19.00, another cyclist found himself face to face with a small man in a diving suit (this evidence, once again, is confirmed by its position on a 'straight line'). He gave a description of the being—about four feet tall, and his legs had no heels (Ezekiel said that their legs were straight and had feet like those of calves), its head was like a huge tuft of hair, with brilliant eyes. The being, or animal, moved about on the road for a short time in front of the 'paralysed' witness, then it disappeared into the nearby forest.

Stories like these, which took place in 1954, caused much amusement and there is nothing surprising in this. There were other stories of celestial visitors and descriptions of them were extremely varied. Mention was made of giants, men made of steel, and even of beautiful beings with an ordinary human appearance. But apart from these descriptions not tallying, we doubt them because none of them are situated on a straight line with other reports of the same day. For this reason we are ignoring them here. So we shall confine ourselves to the case of the little men jogging along on legs without heels, with a face covered with hair and with rounded eyes. Their resemblance with the Cherubim or animals of Ezekiel is undeniable, however, such a similarity, however unlikely, will not raise any enthusiasm in anyone, least of all Aimé Michel, who confines himself to retelling objectively the reports he has examined.

The fear brought on by the sight of the God Pan is well known, it has added the word 'panic' to our vocabulary. Pan was a satyr and the Greeks dreaded meeting him in the loneliness of the woods.

Like the stories of fauns and satyrs, certain genii in Persia are depicted as walking on the feet of cows. In the Islamic tradition certain djinns, the Fis, had 'the figure of a man, the mouth of a dog, the feet of a cow, and the hair of sheep'. They lived, it was said, 'on the third Earth'. [Cf. *Naissance du Monde* (Islam), Edit du Seuil.]

CHAPTER EIGHT

Fatima

WE MUST now take a journey in time and come back from ages long past to arrive unexpectedly in a recent era. We are going to stop at a period not shrouded in the mists of antiquity: the time of the Great War of 1914–18 when almost all humanity was ranged on one side or the other for the first time in history.

Let us look at a small country situated at the extreme south-west of Europe; whose sons were fighting on a distant front on the side of the Allies.

A little village baking in the sun. Three children—two girls and a little boy—looking after a flock. . . .

But let us go straight to the point.

On 13 October 1917 at Fatima in Portugal—where today there is a large church—a huge crowd of curious people, thought to consist of more than 50,000, were gathered to await a wonder visible to everyone. Three little children had declared that a Lady of Light (*uma senhorita de luz*) had been appearing to them regularly for several months and that this wonder had been definitely promised by the Lady. It would take place at mid-day (local time) on this 13 October 'in order that all might believe'.

Thus 50,000 people from all over the country, many

from the capital, Lisbon, waited in driving rain to see if the spectre would appear in a dramatic fashion before the waiting multitudes, or whether nothing would happen at all—which was much more likely.

A little before the appointed hour the rain ceased and the sky began to clear of clouds. When it was exactly mid-day, local time, the three children fell down in ecstasy, and 50,000 or more people saw something that they thought was the sun looking as if it had been 'detached from the sky' and had become like 'a polished silver disc, not blinding bright, with clear-cut edges'. It shuddered, rocked and turned round and round giving off bright lights that changed colour. It stopped turning and then zig-zagged downwards which caused general stupor, and then returned to the sky, where 'it took on its normal appearance', that is to say, it was no longer possible to look at it.

The whole thing had lasted about ten minutes.

Today Fatima has become a centre of pilgrimage which has become famous the world over—it is the rival of Lourdes in France. The basilica welcomes thousands of the faithful every year who have come to worship the Virgin Mary. Cures take place there as well as lasting conversions. It is one of the most important places for Roman Catholics in the twentieth century.

Do not let us make any mistake; all this is momentous.

It is true that the miracle of Fatima is not one of the dogmas that a Roman Catholic is compelled to accept as authentic; indeed, there are many believers who have their own opinions on the subject and on several occasions we have mentioned this subject to priests who, accepting the miracle of Lourdes as a divine manifestation, did not hesitate to consign Fatima to the realm of superstition: but it is a fact that priests who talk like this have studied the facts of the Lourdes story, while they have only learned about Fatima by hearsay.

Nevertheless Fatima is a place where the blind recover their sight, where those who weep are comforted, and where cripples walk. This in itself should lead to respect, or at least discretion, on the subject of suns which dance.

Besides it is far from our thoughts to reduce this 'miracle' to the passing of an ordinary flying saucer—nothing could allow us to dismiss this affair as ordinary. . . . What advantage would be gained by making such a transposition? What would be gained by 'explaining' a miracle, itself something that could not be proved, by the presence of a metallic flying saucer—which is just as difficult to prove as the other? . . . The similarity or dissimilarity in the two cases would not bring us anywhere nearer solving the mystery, it would just be one inexplicable object instead of another.

But the suggestions that we are going to put down follow a completely different train of thought, and it is here more than ever necessary to keep a clear and impartial judgement. Whether you, reader, believe in flying saucers, whether you are indifferent, or whether you are a sceptic, we ask you to follow our chain of reasoning calmly and without prejudice either way. We will see later where our reasoning will take us. It is all quite logical.

Let us first have a look at the story of Fatima from the beginning.

On 13 May 1917—the thirteenth day of the fifth month of the third complete year of the Great War—three little shepherd children, two little girls and one boy, came back from the fields as usual; but on return they told their parents, not without a great deal of stumbling and hesitation, how a 'Lady of Light', of great beauty, had appeared to them above the top of an evergreen oak. The vision had spoken: she asked them to return to the same place on the thirteenth of the following month.

All they received as a result were several vigorous blows

No one had the right to pretend to be Bernadette Soubirous, the saint of Lourdes, especially sixty years afterwards, and it was very disagreeable for the parents of a humble family to find they had children who saw visions. However the good reputation of the children was in their favour and the curiosity of the villagers was roused enough for an escort to follow the children to their rendezvous.

There those who had come were able to watch the children fall on their knees while a faint white vapour formed round them; the daylight as well as the temperature began to lose their intensity and a fresh breeze began to blow. No one saw a 'beautiful Lady' but the eldest of the children, Lucia, talked as if she were speaking to someone and then listened to inaudible replies. The villagers, according to their own words, only heard a soft buzzing. . . . At the moment that Lucia said the 'Lady' was disappearing something happened: the branches of the evergreen oak bent down as if pulled in the direction shown by the little girl.

It was not surprising that on 13 July several hundred people gathered at Cova da Iria, the place where the apparitions took place, to take part in a display which was just like that of the previous month. Lucia declared afterwards that the 'Lady' had confided a certain number of 'secrets' to her. This time the departure of the celestial visitor was accompanied by a sharp report so that a triumphal arch, put up to celebrate the occasion, was shaken on its foundations.

Reaction was not slow in forthcoming. The local governor, disbelieving, wanted to make the children swear that they had made it all up, but all to no avail. He then tried to make them disclose the 'secrets' the 'Lady' had given them, but met with as little success. On 13 August, while a very large crowd made its way to Cova de Iria, he decided to arrest the little promoters of public disorder and took them to the sub-prefecture of police at Ourem, and submitted them to a new interrogation, first together and then separately: he threatened to plunge them into a large pot of boiling oil if they persisted in their silence: 'Your little brother has already been fried!' he said to one of the little girls, who went pale, but continued to remain silent.

While this was taking place the pilgrims assembled at Cova da Iria learned that the children would not be coming. There was first dismay and then anger—certainly the absence of the little shepherds would result in nothing happening. Nevertheless a sort of thunder-clap was heard, like the explosion of a fog-signal, *followed* by a flash of lightning. The white mist rose up from the ground and everything took place as if the children had been there. And it all lasted about ten minutes.

Four days later, the three little children, back at their normal work, suddenly saw the valley light up with the yellow glow that usually preceded the apparitions, and behold, there was the 'Lady'. Lucia threw herself on her knees and besought her to do something that would make those around her believe when she told what she had seen. The 'Lady'—according to Lucia naturally—promised a remarkable sight for October.

But it was only August and an interview took place meanwhile on 13 September. This time 20,000 to 30,000 people were gathered round the children and already the vision was becoming more complex in a striking manner. In addition to the white vapour surrounding the children some of the people there—but not all—saw a luminous globe majestically crossing the sky, coming from the east and making for the evergreen oak. Ten minutes later, the interview over, the same globe reappeared and went off towards the sky. People pointed at it, whilst an old white-haired lady with her missal in her hand, stamped 'I see nothing! I see nothing!'

It was then declared that a large number of white objects, like thin flakes of snow, fell from the sky and disintegrated as soon as they touched the ground.

These are the actual words used by those who witnessed these 'atmospheric phenomena' (that is what they were called) and let us not forget that these witnesses, when they spoke, always thought that they were describing the details of an appearance by the Virgin Mary, from various things they have said.

'To my great surprise,' declared one of these witnesses, 'I saw clearly and distinctly a ball of light sliding slowly and majestically through space. . . . Then suddenly, with the extraordinary light that it let out, this globe disappeared before my eyes, and the priest who was at my side saw it no more either.' When he asked this priest what he thought the globe was, the latter replied without any hesitation, 'that it was without doubt the *craft* in which the Virgin Mary was brought down to her children. . . .

'All those who saw this globe,' another witness said, 'had the impression that it was an *aeroplane of light* bringing the Mother of God to meet the shepherd children and then taking her back to Paradise. . . .'

Let us not try to understand why, in the minds of those gathered there, the Mother of God should have felt the need to use a craft or an aeroplane to come down to Earth. From what we have seen already this idea is nothing short of laughable. Let us remember that despite the absurdity of such a theory, the impression mechanically felt by those who saw the wonder was that of an 'aerial vehicle' and not of a meteor or simple mass hallucination.

That everyone did not see the globe is more disturbing especially that whether or not they saw the object had no bearing on their degree of faith. Perhaps these celestial craft are only visible from certain angles. Or perhaps they are able to implant certain ideas in the minds of certain people. We just do not know. In any case, we can draw the rather disquieting conclusion that craft of this nature are able to fly over our heads without our always being able to see them ourselves.

Let us go on to the shower of white objects: 'Under the wondering eyes [of those present] something like flakes of snow [sic] but round and brilliant came down very slowly towards the ground in a brilliant ray of supernatural light. As if they were drawn to Earth by the irresistible current of a river of light of dazzling brightness, a huge number of white objects like snowflakes drifted down from the sky. They became narrower as one watched them coming down, and disappeared as soon as they touched the ground.'

A lady declared that she had seen these 'flower petals' settle on her left shoulder; she wanted to pick them up but they had vanished.

There were similar showers of white rain at Cova da Iria, especially on 13 May 1918, the anniversary of the first appearance, and on 13 May 1924.

Let us set down at once, to help our memory in connection with what we have just discussed, another account which has nothing to do with the miracles of Fatima; that of another 'rain', no less unusual, which accompanied the flight of a formation of mysterious craft (a cigar and several discs in 1952 in the skies above Oloron, Basses-Pyrénées): 'All these mysterious objects left a considerable trail behind them which drifted slowly down to earth and then disintegrated. For several hours there were tufts of it hanging on trees, telephone wires and roofs of houses.' It was like woollen or nylon thread, like the *Virgin's Hair;* they became gelatinous very quickly and then melted and disappeared. Among the many people who were able to pick them up and hold them in the hand for a moment or two were schoolmasters—one of them examined them carefully, but he was not able to analyse as they had disintegrated before he was able to get them to a laboratory.

The same rain, likened to glass wool or the threads from a spider's web was seen after an appearance of heavenly craft over Graulhet (Tarn) this time on 13 October 1954. And again, on 18 October at Vienne (Isère).... Experts thought about the subject and put forward 'natural' explanations even more astounding because of their inadequacy than the phenomenon itself.

Glass wool, spider's web: these descriptions do not fit

exactly with the 'white corpuscles' which pious prejudice transforms into 'flower petals'. However a certain likeness does remain between these various falls of celestial 'manna' which melt rapidly in meeting the warmth of the ground.

Let us return to Fatima whilst the dawn is breaking on that celebrated 13 October, the date fixed for the appearance of the wonder which was to be the final proof of the truth of the tales of little Lucia. The 'Lady of Light' had promised that after that everyone would be able to believe her. If the wonder took place the little shepherdess had told the truth and had invented nothing.

According to calculations made at the time, between 50,000 and 70,000 people gathered around Cova da Iria. Among this crowd the majority of the people were believers, but in addition were those who were just curious, the sceptics and even anticlerical journalists who had come to jeer at the credulity of the public. One of them, editor-in-chief of the Socialist paper *O Seculo* (*The Century*) gave, as a result, a particularly valuable testimony (in a letter to a fellow-atheist, the Mayor of Santarem) as he was completely impartial.

At 10.00 the sky was covered with black clouds and the rain fell heavily; but nobody thought of going home. Photographs taken on that day graphically show the crowd covered by a forest of umbrellas. A little before the customary time of the appearance of the 'Lady', and although the weather had only slightly improved, Lucia asked people to shut their umbrellas; the request, passed round from mouth to mouth, was rapidly carried out.

At 13.30, official time, but mid-day by local time, the clouds began to disperse. The children fell in ecstasy; the usual white mist formed and rose round them three times. In a few moments Lucia cried out loudly: 'Look at the sun!' Surprised, the people, who had been watching the evergreen oak anxiously in the hope of seeing something or someone, turned round. The wonder that was announced then took place.

'I could see the sun,' wrote one of those present, 'like a disc with sharp edges luminous and brilliant, but not in any way hurtful to the eyes. I heard people comparing it to a disc of matt silver; but I did not think this was quite correct as it was of a brighter colour, vivid and rich, shimmering like a pearl. This disc did not look in the least like the Moon, which looks transparent and pure at night: it looked like *a living star*. It was different from the Moon in another way, it was not spherical, it looked like a flat and polished disc which had been cut from the pearl in a shell ... and was clearly seen to have a ridged edge like a drawing-board.'

But this silvery sun, flat and disc-shaped, could not have been very high up, for in the words of another witness 'the light clouds which crossed the sky from east to west did not hide the brightness of the star and as a result one gained the impression that these clouds passed behind the Sun and not in front of it.' The 'star' was therefore at that moment between the clouds and the Earth.

Suddenly the Sun shuddered and rocked, and then began to turn round and round sending out bundles of light-beams which changed colour at regular intervals. The whole landscape was affected by these colours, 'but *senhora*, you've turned yellow!' cried one of the witnesses, before the lady turned in succession green, blue and then crimson at the same time as everyone else. After two or three minutes, the disc seemed to hang motionless for several seconds, then it began again its gyratory movements, changing colour all the time. Finally, becoming blood-red it began to come down in a series of zig-zagging leaps, each of which brought it nearer the Earth, where the temperature rose sharply. Finally, after a final swing, much more slowly, the disc rose rapidly up to the heavens—at that moment completely bare of clouds. Then everything suddenly reverted to normal; the Sun, motionless in the sky shone with its customary dazzling light, preventing the crowd from looking at it any further.

78

The clothes of those who, since the morning, had been drenched by the rain were now completely dry.

The accounts and testimonies which we have just told, can be found almost exactly the same in the books devoted to the appearances at Fatima. Take, for example, *Fatima, Espérance du Monde,* by G. Renault (Editions Plon), a study composed of photographs taken at the time of the event, on 13 October 1917, as well as reproductions of articles from contemporary journals.

While the details of the 'dance of the Sun' as told to us by witnesses are fresh in our mind, let us compare them with more recent sightings of 'unidentified flying objects'; perhaps we shall be no longer astonished to find that they coincide exactly.

Fatima (extracts from officially confirmed reports)	*Flying Saucer Sightings* (from Aimé Michel and Donald Keyhoe)
A disc with sharp edges, at the edge bright, luminous, and brilliant, but not tiring the eyes at all.	A luminous disc as large as the full Moon, but shining with a brighter glow was hanging motionless in the night sky. Suddenly the object began to rock.... (A baker from Arras, 1954).
I heard people compare it with a matt silver disc, but this did not seem accurate to me as it seemed to have a brighter, more vivid and richer colour like the sheen of a pearl.	The object was lit-up by a pale light, not blinding, rather like that of neon. (The crew of a French Air Force plane, 1954).
This pearly disc was moving at a dizzy speed. It was not the twinkling of a star: it	It was a wheel looking as if it had been made of red-hot iron, turning round. (The

79

turned round at an astounding speed.

It was suddenly transformed into a wheel of fire. The sun threw bundles of rays of blue, red, violet, yellow and green light in all directions.

Suddenly detached from the sky, the sun seemed to rebound in the sky by a series of leaps and bounds. . . . It approached by a series of zig-zag movements.

As if hesitating, the sun paused before going, recalled by a mysterious order taking its place high in the heavenly vault.

The clothes of those who since the morning had been drenched by the rain were now completely dry.

crew of an air-liner of TWA in the USA in 1952).

Shining first with an intense blue, the object soon changed to white, while a red halo appeared at its edges. The object revolves with a rapid motion. (Sighting at Dole (Jura) in 1954). Above Phoenix (Arizona) the craft changed successively from red to green then from yellow to blue. (1952).

When the craft began to come down, it began to shake like a dead leaf, like the movement of a pendulum. Then it hung in the sky turning like a top. (Lieut. J. Kilburn on board a jet aircraft, September 1952).

The final descent was like that of a dead leaf, but after hanging for a moment like a pendulum, the craft shot upwards at an angle, and disappeared. (Le Bourget, 1952).

After the passage of a craft giving off intense heat a log merchant from Lusigny, near Troyes, declared that despite the rain, the ground and the trees were as dry as if the sun were shining. (20 October, 1954).

It is hardly reasonable to assume that those who told these tales, describing heavenly objects ten years ago had been influenced by the memory of earlier tales, for the simple reason that most of them would never have heard of them.

The events at Fatima took place at a time when the pages of the newspapers were almost entirely given up to the development of military operations, and the news from the war fronts left little space for other news, especially when it took place in an obscure village lost in the heart of Portugal. Very few people in the world took the trouble at the time to ask what had happened in Fatima. Later, the pilgrimages drew the attention of journalists, but their accounts remained concise. It is therefore not possible to pretend that the descriptions given above had even vague memories as their origin: among a hundred people chosen at random, how many would really be able to give precise details of the famous 'dance of the Sun'.

It is after all remarkable that no one has openly made any comparison like this before. Perhaps it may have been done secretly, but the person who did it took care not to make any statement about it in public lest he be thought to be sliding down a slippery path.

However, those who take some sort of interest in the wonders of Cova da Iria did little afterwards in the way of enquiry to see what exactly did happen.

No observatory on our planet, we are sure, noticed anything unusual about the behaviour of the Sun on that 13 October 1917: the daystar had not really 'danced', not thrown off sparks, nor changed colour. However, there are a certain number of well-intentioned people who declare that the Sun really did dance that day, but that the miracle consisted merely in that no observatory noticed it. . . . Needless to say that this idea does not have many followers, even among the faithful.

81

The believers in Fatima object that nothing can substantiate the particularly unusual form which this so-called hallucination took. Indeed those who were present at Cova da Iria were so inclined to expect something unusual that they were waiting for something to appear like the Virgin Mary, Jesus Christ, or even the Holy Family together, or perhaps to witness a further shower of flower petals or several other phenomena in connection with the previous appearances; while they were waiting they were all looking in the direction of the evergreen-oak the place where the other manifestations had taken place. When Lucia cried 'Look at the Sun!' not a single person present would have expected such an amazing sight, even less been able to tell the other members of the crowd that such an unexpected sight would take place. In any case, the crowd, in order to 'see' the dancing Sun, had to turn its back on the evergreen oak.

If this psychological argument is not enough for those who declare that the whole thing was a mass hallucination, there is an even more convincing one. A mile or two from Cova da Iria there is a village, whose inhabitants were going about their daily tasks on 13 October 1917 and were not among the crowds so were not in the right place to see the 'hallucination'. But their attention was drawn to the unusual sight of a bright disc in motion and they were able to watch it from a distance. They all met together in the centre of the village, wondering what was the meaning of the sight.

But if it is thought probable that a collective hallucination could affect every single member of a crowd made up of more than 50,000 people in the same place as they were all expecting the same thing, it is a very different matter when two crowds several miles apart see the object, especially when one of the crowds was not expecting anything unusual at all. In such a case even scientists would admit that this was hardly likely to be a case of mass hallucination.

We are left with the possibility that the pilgrims to Cova da Iria really did see 'something', which they wrongly thought was the Sun, appear in the sky, or more correctly, between the sky and the clouds which made such odd movements.

It is very tempting to stop at this point and say 'Look here, it is obvious, the crowd mistook a flying saucer for the Sun. It is therefore no miracle, for the appearance of an unidentified flying object cannot be called a miracle'. But do we know as much as that? We do not know how miracles work, but neither do we know any more about flying saucers, therefore it is pointless to replace one by the other and we are just as wise as we were before.

Unfortunately it is not as easy as all that.

It is impossible to draw conclusions so soon because, whether we like it or not the manoeuvres of the object above Cova da Iria cannot be separated from their religious context.

The wonder that occurred in that place, at the time forecast, exactly as was said by the three small visionaries, demonstrated their complete sincerity; the children could have invented everything except that. Even the theory that a space craft had flown over Cova da Iria by chance, drawn by the sight of the large crowd will not hold water; as it does not explain the other phenomena, less grand in scale, which had already taken place on the thirteenth of the previous month. The repetition of such a 'coincidence' after a month's interval to the very day does not belong to the realm of coincidence.

So we are forced to admit that there is some connection between the forecasts of the children and their fulfilment. And as it would be impossible for them, almost two months in advance, to know on their own account, the exact day the occurrence would take place, we have to conclude that they were warned. From this we see that there must have been some connection between the contact with the children and those who arranged the 'wonder'. There must have been some collusion between the children and their visitor; and the words which they uttered and which called the crowd together must have been dictated to them.

By whom?

By someone or something which looked to them like a 'Lady of Light' and this 'Lady' spoke. She even spoke Portuguese—unless she spoke by telepathy and even then her ideas were put into words without difficulty by the children. . . . And even if she did come from 'heaven', according to their own words, or at least another world, she knew the variations of our western calendar well enough not to make a mistake between the months with thirty-one and those with thirty days. The rendezvous was always fixed for the thirteenth of each month.

Even better, this 'Lady of Light' was clearly knowledgable about the religious beliefs of the little Portuguese children, since she talked to them along the lines of their beliefs. . . . She pretended to call herself Our Lady of the Rosary, and talked of her Son, 'who was shocked by the sins of the world' and gave out edifying sermons, recommending repentance, penitence and prayer.

It is clear that there exists a connection that is quite clear between the object that resembled a luminous 'Lady' (seen by very few people), that other thing which appeared in the form of a coloured disc (visible to very many more people), and lastly, the spreading of a certain moral doctrine: a doctrine which we shall see cannot just be taken as a matter of course.

Little Lucia, who is still alive today, did indeed put into practice the advice which was lavished on her: she is a nun in a convent in Italy; and celebrated her fiftieth birthday in 1957.

The two other little shepherds died very young as a result of the epidemic of Spanish influenza.

CHAPTER NINE

Interlude

IT IS perhaps a good time to stop for a while in order to take stock of what we have discussed so far. Before making further discoveries and drawing our conclusions from them, let us cast a rapid glance over the road we have travelled already.

(1) The idea that life exists outside the Earth is in accordance with the opinion of present-day science.

There is nothing to justify the opinion to the contrary—that the Earth is alone and unique in this way among an abundance of solar systems.

(2) That life outside the Earth could develop intelligent beings, and indeed of the highest intelligence, is in accordance with the opinions of present-day science.

We have no reason to believe that human development represents a culmination of all development; a swift examination of our own level of development and that of those entities like us does a lot to make us feel modest. It is probable that other places in the universe have produced beings who have passed us in scientific, technical and psychological knowledge.

(3) The realisation that interplanetary distances can be crossed is in accordance with the opinion of present-day science.

This idea is a complete novelty, and our minds have not had the time to get used to it and to think calmly about its consequences.

Our timid beginnings in space travel, which remind us of the first crossing of the English Channel by an aircraft, open the way to space for us. The exploration of the solar system will be able to be undertaken from Earth in a few years time—technicians vie with us in telling us this, and political leaders repeat it after them.

So if journeys from the Earth to outer space are possible, so are journeys in the other direction. Thus it is a scientific conclusion that it would be possible for entities from outer space to visit our planet.

The speed of evolution is not necessarily the same all over the universe, other beings might be a million or a thousand million years in advance of us.

To declare categorically that this is true falls in the sphere of science fiction, but to admit that it is a possibility comes in the realm of science proper.

However, here we must leave the realm of scientific opinion and instead turn back the pages of history.

(4) In every age and in almost every part of the world men have confirmed that they have seen luminous craft, tubular or circular, travelling across the sky or even making contact with the soil of our Earth.

The event was always reported as quite a rare fact, although it took place at long intervals all down the ages, following an irregular pattern.

Some people declared that they were celestial craft, others that they came from the gods (*deus ex machina*). (This last expression was often used in the ancient theatre. Many situations there included the appearance of a 'god'; and he was then represented as coming down from the sky by a flying 'machine', suspended, of course, on wires.) The appearance of these craft had repercussions on the religious views and customs of the people they visited.

86

Not only religious either, but technical as well: we can thus explain the spread of certain knowledge which was well in advance of the intellectual level of our ancestors. To take only two cases, mentioned already: the astronomical science of the Chaldeans who had no telescopes, and the knowledge of the properties of naphtha or native petrol among the 'initiates' in Asia Minor.

Other authors mention the discovery in the ruins of Niniveh objects in every respect similar to electric batteries (cf. S. Hutin, *Les Civilisations Inconnues*, ed. A. Fayard and L. Pauwels and J. Bergier, *Le Matin des Magiciens*, ed. Gallimard). On the other hand many passages in the Old Testament make one think that the Ark of the Covenant, brought from Sinai in the care of the Hebrew priests was an accumulator of electric energy whose discharges caused terrible results. Indeed outside the Levites, probably insulated by the special clothing that the Law instructed them to wear, whoever touched the Ark (even if it were for a good purpose, such as in the case of a certain Uzzah who wished to prevent it being upset under the dust of a team of oxen, I Samuel vi, 3–8) was instantly struck dead 'by the anger of Yahveh'. Besides, the presence of the Ark, which was perhaps radioactive, in the midst of Philistines, who had not been immunised, made strange tumours appear on their skin. (I Samuel v.)

We shall soon discover in ancient texts precise information to the fact that certain ancestral industries had been established among men as a result of information supplied by visitors from another stock.

(5) During the recent past metallic and luminous craft, whose origin and nature are unknown, have been sighted thousands of times. This has provoked world-wide interest, leading to the appointment of commissions officially charged by governments and military staff to study the phenomena scientifically.

There has been every sort of suggestion made in an

attempt to solve the mystery. Hoaxes, mistakes, optical illusions, collective hallucination, confusion with ballon-sondes have been put forward as solutions. The spherical form of ballon-sondes, and their occasional brightness owing to reflection have often given rise to false reports. Aimé Michel gives the case of one of these balloons, sent out by an Italian observatory, which drifted with the wind for three days over the sky of southern France. Many people thought they had seen a flying saucer when they observed it and sent in detailed accounts. It is remarkable that these reports, far from giving details added by the imagination, were excellent descriptions of the ballon-sonde: this goes to show that reports sent in by the public are not as inaccurate as might be supposed.

It is worth noting, too, that the paths of ballon-sondes, always changing because of the wind, never remain in a straight line for long; neither are the places from which they are observed in a straight line either. (Cf. Aimé Michel, *Mystérieux Objets Célestes*).

But none of the solutions put forward to explain the mystery of the flying saucers takes all the circumstances into account. The presence of luminous blips on radar screens which corresponded with the actual appearance of the craft in the sky is another factor in favour of the reality of flying saucers.

The only possible explanation, that these craft are inter-planetary, which for the moment, cannot be proved, has been rejected as if it was no real explanation.

Lastly, the absence of formal proof, together with the decrease in the rate of sightings has led to a diminution of interest in the whole matter and people tend now to take the view that they are a myth without foundation in fact.

Let us remember the phenomenon of 'mental blockage', or unconscious inhibition, resulting from the fear of seeing all the current scientific theories collapse. This, according to Arthur Koestler, is like the attitude of the scientist of the sixteenth and seventeenth centuries towards the discoveries of Copernicus, Kepler and Galileo. (Cf. pp. 31–32.)

Nevertheless, those who have had the chance to study, as objectively as possible, the details of the events that have been described (even if they do not examine the file in full to see for themselves the absurdity of the theory that the whole thing is hallucination), have finished by being convinced that the craft that have been seen are certainly real —whatever they are.

Finally, the discovery of the fact that the people who see these craft, when there are enough of them in number, are not scattered about haphazardly, but always along straight lines when plotted on the map, should be enough to remove all final doubts. Certainly, this does not explain anything, but it does rule out the hypothesis of chance coincidence— and that is going a long way.

(6) If there are striking similarities between present-day descriptions of unidentified craft, and those which took place in ages gone by, it is more than a similarity, but descriptions of the same craft and this is especially true of the events at Fatima.

Indeed, the terms used to describe the solar wonder of 1917 are not only similar, but exactly the same as the descriptions given of the appearance and behaviour of flying saucers.

Psychiatry is unable to prove the possibility of such consistency in a collective hallucination affecting people healthy in mind and of very different psychological temperaments: thus a level-crossing keeper, opening his window because a light, reflected on the walls of his room woke him up with a start, noticing a bright craft on the railway line at Londe (Seine Maritime) on 18 November 1960 (Cf. *Figaro* for 19 November 1960), an astronomer observing through his telescope the presence of an orange circular object which was motionless (i.e. moving at a speed equal to the rotation of the Earth)—this happened several times at Armentières the most notable occasion being on 30 June 1961 (Journal of the Astronomical Association of the North of France), none of the satellites launched before that date by the Americans or the Russians had taken up a position above a point on the Earth, and finally a pilgrim come to see a wonder which had been forecast two months earlier—are all in spheres of life that are completely different.

The theory that symbolic images occur again and again in the collective memory of humanity (archtypes) can explain the repetition of the same kind of dream and the visions of people suffering from cerebral lesions, but cannot be brought forward to explain the *concrete* facts which surround the mystery of the flying saucers. These include the quality of the reports, the mass of technical detail whose description does not tally in the least with the 'archtypes', the blips on radar screens monitored by soldiers, and lastly, the sightings occurring in straight lines. (We are careful not to mention in this list any photographs of saucers as their authenticity is always open to suspicion: if Professor Jung makes great play with this fact it can be more than offset by the radar blips, the telescope sightings, and the appearance of the craft in straight lines).

As a result of the first three propositions, it is more in accord with the scientific approach to conclude that the answer is an invasion of beings from outer space and to reject any other explanations, which are much less satisfactory.

Thus the Sun which the Portuguese saw dancing at Fatima was very similar in all respects to one of the flying discs whose sporadic visits to the neighbourhood of our Earth has been reported by men all down the ages.

Its outward appearance, as well as the way it shook, its zig-zag descent, its remarkable departure are all characteristics which have been seen on sightings of flying saucers. There is nothing to distinguish the sighting at Cova da Iria from many other sightings of 'unidentified flying objects' in the middle of the twentieth century except for the unique fact that this sighting was announced in advance, which resulted in a vast crowd gathering in order to see it.

More than this, the advance publicity which was accompanied by wonders of a less sensational nature, just as a parade of animals is made as advance publicity for a circus, took place in a context that was entirely religious.

The nebulous being who played the part of intermediary between that other world and ours appeared to the three little shepherds under the name of 'Our Lady', that is to say, Mary, the Mother of Jesus of Nazareth—someone from the Bible. From this fact, and from the essentially religious nature of the message given, the appearances at Fatima are directly connected with similar incidents which are described in Scripture.

If the beings who commanded—or telecommanded—the craft of this nature had been the same, or more or less the same, types and from the same origin as those that had appeared earlier to encourage the prophets—as well as the first Christian Apostles (which we shall see later) one can only marvel at their constancy and the similarity of the messages. . . .

And in the same way, certain similarities between the 'animals' described by Ezekiel, following other traditions, and the 'little men' who were seen for brief moments in our day on points situated on the tell-tale straight lines, tend to show that we have always been visited by the same kind of thing—more or less—presumably with the same objects in view.

This is, admittedly a prejudice, which naturally does not exclude the possibility of completely different aims, about which we know absolutely nothing. For what purpose, for example, are the coloured projections of the 'jelly-fish', pointing towards the soil? Probably for something completely different than for the spreading of a metaphysical message. But we must not speculate aimlessly about this as it could not have much success, since all that we know

91

about our visitors from outer space is what it has pleased them to reveal to us.

But this does not prevent us from playing a game, an intellectual bet.

There is, if everything that we have said so far is true, something very important; something, perhaps that is tragic.

In 1919 an American, Charles Fort, after carefully collecting press cuttings about strange facts which science could not explain, ended by believing that we are spied upon, watched, guided and even given telepathic commands. In a style written in the blackest humour, Fort thus explains his fears:

'Pigs, geese, and cows have first of all to find out who possesses them, and then to worry about why they own them. Perhaps we, too, can be used?'

The author goes on to suggest that our species had been the subject of contracts and agreements between many people, who shared the benefits of our exploitation. Our masters, he thought, followed one after the other in using us:

'Something has a legal right over us, obtained by force, after having paid to obtain it, the equivalent in beads which our previous proprietor had paid before, who was more primitive.' And he adds this, which is very important: 'And this transaction [between successive owners] has been known for many centuries by some among us, whose members, as first-class slaves, order us in accordance with instructions received and direct us to our mysterious tasks.' (From the *Book of the Damned*, chapter XII). When Charles Fort wrote these lines, he showed that he had ideas which are not ours, and we think we should go into more detail. But it is significant that the author of the *Book of the Damned* had been led, by a very different path from that which we have followed, to suggest solutions that are not unlike those we shall put forward in the second part of this work—even if, in spite of undoubted similarities—we remain in disagreement with him about the basis of the problem.

92

CHAPTER TEN

From Washington to the Vatican

IT WAS a little after midnight on 20 July 1952, when the technicians at the Air Traffic Control Center at Washington, saw a set of blips appear on their radar screens which carried out a series of unusual evolutions over the capital of the United States and which continued to do so until dawn. At first there were seven 'blips' which fascinated the men in charge, among them Senior Controller Harry G. Barnes, Controller Jim Ritchley, James Copeland, and Ed. Nugent. The craft appeared at a fantastic speed, and then suddenly slowed down and massed to the south-west of the station. From the top of the control tower one of the operators made out the form of a very brilliant orange light.

The technicians telephoned the radar centre of the Air Force at Andrews Field in Maryland on the other side of the river Potomac. There they had also made out the 'objects' and they were busy following their strange evolutions. At that moment they were spread out; two of them were flying over the White House, a third was over the Capitol, both places over which flying was not allowed. A third radar centre, which looked after the local services, noticed these craft as well.

Their average speed was estimated at 130 miles per hour, a reasonable speed, but during several remarkable manoeuvres, during which the observers saw them make rapid movements which took them to another part of the sky: it was worked out that these leaps were at speeds equivalent to approximately 6,000 miles per hour, a speed quite unknown at that time. This speed was confirmed by the radar screens.

In normal circumstances the officials would have ordered up several jet fighters to intercept these ill-timed visitors, but by chance, the runway at Andrews Field was under repair which made it unusable at that time and the air squadron had been transferred temporarily to Newcastle: it would take half an hour for the aircraft to reach Washington. But two hours passed before they arrived and rumour said that this was caused by another alert of the same order coming from the New York area. Several minutes before the jet aircraft came into sight, the luminous craft disappeared from the radar screens. The disappointed airmen returned to their base. Then the mysterious craft reappeared once more, and continued their evolutions.

However, several air liners left the civil airport and others landed there; their pilots and their passengers distinctly saw the orange lights in the night sky while the men at the control towers observed them also through the eyepieces of their theodolites. The pilots of one of the craft tried to approach one of these craft, causing it to streak away.

The tournament in space continued until the dawn began to appear on the horizon, then everything reverted to normal: there were only the stars in the sky getting ever paler.

The staff of the Air Force did all they could to find an explanation of these incidents which would set people's minds at rest. First they tried a simple denial, then they had to admit the truth of the sightings, too many people had talked about what they had seen before they received the order to keep silent on the subject. Letters, telegrams and telephone calls showered into the Pentagon asking for an official explanation. Some people thought they were secret craft sent by a hostile power—but it was well known in high places that no earthly technique was capable of producing craft capable of similar manoeuvres or of such speeds. A much larger number of people began to consider seriously the possibility of interplanetary invasion.

But this is just what the government of the United States wanted to avoid at all cost, knowing by experience how easily such a rumour could cause a national or even international panic. They recalled the radio programme by Orson Welles, inspired by H. G. Wells, about a landing of Martians on the Earth, and which, taken as news by some of those who listened to it, let loose much disorder in several American cities.

Journalists asked for a press conference, increasing their demands as the accounts of the sightings began to come in from all sides; not only in the United States, but also from the rest of the world. According to the London *Sunday Graphic* a disc about forty-five feet in diameter had been taken by surprise in a forest clearing near Hasselbach in East Germany; at the approach of witnesses two silhouettes dressed in something metallic took refuge in the craft. The craft glowed red and took off vertically. In many places radar confirmed visual sightings, and the tension grew to an intolerable level.

The conference the press demanded took place at the Pentagon, on 29 July, that is, nine days after the events at Washington. General Samford was in the chair and he was accompanied by experts from the Air Technical Intelligence Centre: Col. Donald L. Bower, Captain Ed. Ruppelt, Captain Roy L. James—and supported by the Chief of Air Defense, Major-General Roger M. Ramey.

The brass-hats of the Air Force were very reticent, parrying the questions put to them, refusing to commit themselves, and succeeded in killing the rumours. The meeting ended with the impression that it would be expedient to attribute the sightings of the night of 20 July to an optical illusion that was common enough, arising from a 'temperature inversion' like the mirages in the desert.

This 'solution' which seemed to please everyone as it permitted the journalists to write articles on it, did not take
account of a certain number of facts which completely contradicted it—among others that the atmospheric conditions
recorded by the meterological office at Washington were not
nearly high enough to cause such mirages. After all, the
technicians at the radar control centres knew the causes of
temperature inversions too well to have confused them with
the wave of sightings; they all declared that the images
produced on their screens by phenomena of this nature
bore no resemblance to what they had seen on the night of
20 July 1952.

Thus the mystery remained complete: for many Ameri-
can citizens the embarrassed replies of the leaders of the
American Air Force seemed merely cowardly escapism.
The impression that visitors from outer space had entered
the skies of our planet convinced more and more people.
Among those who were won over to this idea were even
certain people holding high positions on the staff of the Air
Force itself.

The detailed story of the events that took place and the
report of the press conference of 29 July 1952 as well as the
photographic facsimile of the certificate of authenticity coming from the Department of Defense, Office of Public Information, Washington, DC, can be found in *Flying Saucers
From Outer Space* by the journalist Donald Keyhoe (Hutchinson, London).

On the other hand the accuracy of the report had been
openly recognised—despite a certain ironical reserve about
the natural tendency of a journalist to add colour to his
stories—by Captain Ed. Ruppelt, whose name appeared on
the list of people appearing at the press conference at the
side of General Samford as we have mentioned above. We
have also mentioned his book, *Report on UFO*.

Two years previously, Pope Pius XII was favoured on

several occasions by a most unexpected vision while walking in the gardens of the Vatican. Let us read the words of Cardinal Tedeschini, who gave an account of the event to the world:

'The Sovereign Pontiff, much troubled and very moved as I have never seen him moved before [. . .] honoured me with the confidence which follows: "Yesterday I saw a wonder which made a great impression on me." And later on he told me how he had seen the sun and in what form [. . .].

' "It was 30 October 1950, two days before the Assumption into heaven of the Very Blessed Virgin Mary. At about four o'clock in the afternoon I was taking my usual walk in the gardens of the Vatican, reading and studying various papers as I usually did. [. . .] Raising my eyes from the papers I was holding I saw a phenomenon the like of which I had never seen before. The sun, which was still very high, appeared as an opaque globe, a pale yellow, completely surrounded by a circle of light but which was not so bright that it made it impossible to look at it. There was a small cloud in front of it, very tenuous. The edge of the opaque globe was moving slightly, either turning or moving from left to right. But the centre of the globe was seen to be moving very clearly and without interruption. The same phenomenon was repeated the next day, 31 October, and on 1 November, the feast-day, and then 8 November, its octave. After that, nothing. Many times I have looked at the same time on other days in identical atmospheric conditions to see if the same phenomenon would occur, but in vain: I have not seen the sun except in its usual dazzling brightness." ' (Quoted in *Fatima, Espérance du Monde* by G. Renault, Editions Plon.)

To obtain the effect described, a disc-shaped space ship would have to put itself—when it was far enough from our globe—as nearly as possible on the Sun-Earth axis. At that moment the craft would be completely invisible to us, lost in the intense brilliance of the Sun's rays, which are too strong

for us to look at. It could then approach without fear of
attracting our attention until, owing to perspective, its disc
had reached the exact dimension of the solar disc. It would
then form a kind of total eclipse substituting its own
luminous surface, iridescent and slightly amber in colour
for that of the sun, whose rays would make something like
a corona round it. The effect produced would be, for us,
that of a very pale star, not blinding, which we could look
upon without fatigue. If the craft wobbled slightly or re-
volved it would seem to us the Sun danced. In no other
way could this effect be obtained, for it is impossible for
us to look at the Sun for more than a fraction of a second
without having to look away. This phenomenon is what
Pius XII saw in his garden.

It might be worth while, before ending this chapter, to
compare this phenomenon with that of Fatima. According
to the editor of *O Seculo* 'it did not burn anything, it blinded
no one—people said it was an eclipse'. 'It was wonderful'
wrote in his turn, *Senhor* de Almeida Garrett, another witness of the wonder, 'that it was possible to look on the star
for so long without any effect on the eyes. With the exception of two brief moments when the Sun shot forth brilliant
rays violently, which made everyone turn away. ...' etc.

CHAPTER ELEVEN

The Dawn of the World

THE STUDY of fossils has taught us about the slow evolution of the Earth and the development of the living beings upon its surface. We know almost exactly the age of our planet, subject only to any revelations that further discoveries might make. The Earth is about four thousand million years old and life first began here about one thousand million years ago; and the appearance of man is comparatively recent, a mere one million years ago. These are, of course, not definite figures and new discoveries cause scientists to modify their estimates continually.

We know that this evolution was marked with terrestrial upheavals, by the raising of ranges of mountains, and by the depression of continents; and that these cataclysms were caused by an amazing amount of potential energy.

But these ideas, relatively recent in our minds in their scientific form, were already known to our ancestors in their essential form. Indeed, they did not attach as much importance as we do to the number of zeros which appeared in their numbers, and they thought it more practical to express a stretch of time of a thousand million years as 'That lasted a very long time indeed'.

Thus, the idea that man had come late on to our ageing planet is already found expressed in an ancient Islamic parable:

'The Earth said to Adam, when he was created: "O Adam, you come to me when I have lost my freshness and my youth".'

The poetic lack of precision of our fathers takes nothing away from the depth of their thoughts. Indeed, they had certain advantages over us. The whole history is not necessarily recorded in fossil structure, which is the only evidence that science gives us to rebuild our distant past: there may have been events which left no physical trace, and which we have continued to ignore as we have not been able to improve our methods of investigation.

The ancients did not investigate the ground below them, but they depended on traditions handed down from father to son. They had no other sources of information and they also attached great importance to oral evidence. Frequently this evidence seemed to come from a non-human origin, especially in that which concerned terrestrial evolution *before* the appearance of man.

These ideas which had been collected and carefully protected from oblivion ended by forming a Gnosis, from Greek *gnosis*, knowledge, which our ancestors respected as much as we respect science today.

Knowledge and understanding are two complementary ways to take in the world around us. Our ancestors were familiar with the past without being fully able to understand it. Science today can understand it but lack the personal connection our ancestors knew.

What a growth of understanding would be ours if we agreed to work these two methods together!

By limiting ourselves to underlying notions which we can examine ourselves, the idea that before the birth of the human race there was 'nobody' on the Earth seems to be true.

This was not at all the idea of our ancestors, who claimed that our planet had been sown and cultivated by successive waves of extra-terrestrial colonists grouped in hostile bands and often fiercely antagonistic.

The recent suggestion by the scientist who, at Los Angeles, declared that light might have been introduced on to our planet by a space craft erred on the cautious side in the view of our ancestors. They envisaged several space craft and not a single one; craft whose crews were made up like pirates, disputing violently over who was to govern the Earth, causing great harm to the creatures who had settled on our soil. The majority of ancient documents, from wherever they come, are in agreement on this point.

It is expedient to put aside completely the Biblical account of the creation of the world, that is to say, the planning and ordering of the Earth as told in the beginning of Genesis. It is completely unique to present this creation as a peaceful work of a single God. This God was probably situated far above all the strife and tumult and was un-affected by it. After all, the time had not yet arrived when the church compelled the faithful to believe in the story of the six-day creation to the letter: the believer could interpret it as he liked. The encyclical *Humani Generis,* from Pope Pius XII, in 1950, merely recommended that those who tried to explain and interpret the Scriptures, never to lose sight of the fact that if the writers who had composed the Scriptures had borrowed from popular tradition here and there, 'they made their choice of these documents as a result of divine inspiration'.

It is indeed possible that the Yahvist and Elohist tradi-tions were deliberately mutilated following the directives of the 'heavenly guides' of the Hebrews, who doubtless had most respectable motives for suppressing the disorders which had occurred when they established themselves on our planet. . . .

There is nothing of this in the other traditions of the time: the reasons for this will appear to us, on their own

101

account later with regard to the objectives of both sides, which did not coincide in any way at all.

In the accounts coming from all parts of the world quarrels and conflict are related without any hesitation. Much is said of the trouble caused by the furious combats, to which the convulsions of the Earth's crust furnish a parallel upheaval.

A Gnosis in the Mediterranean area shows that the world, that is to say the Earth, had been created by a certain Ialdabaoth, an incapable demi-god, 'who was taken for God' (J. Doresse, *Les livres secrets des gnostiques d'Egypte*, Editions Plon). After repeated evidence of his clumsiness his son snatched the sceptre from him by force in order to reign in his turn and redress the wrongs of his father. This son, whose name was Sabaoth, reigned from then onwards high in the skies. (This tradition has left traces even in the Roman Catholic liturgy, where in the Mass occurs the phrase '*Sanctus, sanctus, sanctus Dominus Deus Sabaoth, pleni sunt coeli et terra gloria tua.*') (Holy, Holy, Holy, Lord God of Sabaoth, Heaven and Earth are full of thy glory.) In the book of Common Prayer the word 'Sabaoth' has been replaced by 'hosts' in the Holy Communion Service.

Besides, the Bible refers to this preliminary struggle in several of its books, a proof that the prophets themselves did not take the version given by Genesis to be absolutely accurate. Isiah (li. 9) mentions 'ancient times', when Yahveh had to slay Rahab, also Leviathan, the dragon; Job mentions this too (xxvi, 13) and it also appears in the Psalms, (lxxiv, xiv and lxxxix, x).

This combat, which preceded and confirmed the sovereignty of Yahveh on the Earth, comes in the Judeo-Christian tradition as the struggle between the archangel St Michael (Hebrew, the man who is like God) and the Dragon. (Cf. *Theologie du Judéo-christianisme*, by R. P. Danielou, Editions Desclée.)

In India, the *Bhagavata Purana* shows us Vishnu, the *Prajapati* (creator) producing not the Light as the Biblical

Elohim ('Let there be light') but thick darkness, error and obscurity. 'Then,' adds the text, 'having contemplated his faulty Creation the Creator could only have a poor opinion of himself' ... (It is a long way from this dramatic dissatisfaction to the contentment of the God of Genesis: 'And God looked and saw that it was good.') Thus to make up for such a sad beginning Vishnu delegated the 'Wise Men' to continue creation in his place. But the 'Wise Men' forgot themselves in sedentary contemplation and created nothing at all. To put an end to this inaction, a young, red god, flame-coloured who sprang up out of the anger of the *Prajapati*, went on with creation and made the first human beings.

The Aztecs, in their turn, attributed the first creation to a couple, Ometecuhli and Omeciuatl, soon dethroned by younger gods more active and more enterprising.

In Assyria the disputes among the first gods were accompanied by shouts and cries which filled the universe and which made the mountains crumble away in terror.

We hear the same idea from Greece, where a very clear legend comes to us, relatively easy to decipher:

Ouranos (or Uranus—the Sky, Space)—fertilises his wife Rhea—the Earth: so let us understand that life on the Earth had a spatial origin. But from this union were born horrible monsters which their horrified father drove back into the womb of their mother, in other words they were 'buried', which permits us to discover them today below our soil, in the form of fossils. . . .

But time (Kronos or Chronos—Saturn to the Romans) put an end to this reign of terror. Ouranos was defeated and Kronos was installed in his place. But Time 'devoured his own works' and everything stultified into a sterile routine. (And the 'Wise Men', forgetting themselves in sedentary contemplation and created nothing at all.) Nevertheless, during that period of stagnation things balanced themselves gradually and a certain order was established, time had as sister harmony—Aphrodite to the Greeks and Shrî to the

Hindus who attributed a role to this goddess in creation equal to the original gods before their fall.

Finally it is the landing in force of a new team of gods led by Zeus (Jupiter or Yod-pater) with whom all the traditions associate dynamism and youth. Their attributes, in Greece as everywhere else, were synonymous with light, speed and power: fire, thunder, whiteness, sunlight, the eagle. Zeus, like the Latin *deus*, is derived from the root *di*, which is found in the words diurnal and divine. He is the equivalent of the Red Child of India, the solar Ormazd of the Persians (conqueror of Ahriman), of the archangel Michael of the Hebrews (conqueror of the dragon).

From then onwards there is a new creation whose object is man.

We today, living in the twentieth century, with our weakness for dates, are able as a result to estimate that this last invasion, which preceded the appearance of man a little, took place about a million years ago.

Does this mean that at the beginning of the new reign everything was calm and peaceful? Not at all, other dissentions arose because of this new creature man whose arrival did not seem desirable to everyone.

An account written in the margin of the Koran by a certain Abu Zayd Al-Bali gives us an insight into the minds of our predecessors:

'I intended,' said God, 'to set up a Caretaker (thus he designated man).

But the angels, companions, of Iblis, then called Azazil, replied: 'Art thou going to place someone on the Earth who will bring in corruption and shed blood when we have not ceased to sanctify Thee?'

But God replied: 'I know that you do not understand.'

(From *La Naissance du Monde 'Islam'*, Editions du Seuil, Collection of Oriental Science.)

It is now our turn to have recourse to a parable.

There is nothing that would give us a better idea of the way that these events took place in ancient times than to look for a similar event in the near future: let us imagine that the day is at hand when the Earthmen of the future, having mastered the art of interplanetary travel and made new biological discoveries undertook the development of another planet (let us say, for convenience, Venus). The reader must pardon our burst of fantasy, as reality at first always seems very like fiction.

When the first Earthly astronauts, having pierced the thick layer of clouds which keep the surface of Venus permanently in semi-darkness, landed on the planet and found it full of life and seething with repugnant animals. They were not long in finding out that they were not the first to land there—for many centuries Venus had belonged to emissaries from Saturn who in their turn had succeeded the original pioneers from Uranus. A handful of Saturnians still carried out vague functions, made even more vague by the slowness of their reactions and the indestructible stubbornness which formed the dominant trait in their character....

The spirit of colonisation which had disappeared from the Earth for a long time suddenly arose once more in our fellow men except that it was no longer confined to their own world but to a planet still only half developed on which almost nothing took place outside the swarming animal life.

The explosion of several new weapons blew up the works of the Saturnians and completely destroyed them. Only a few small mammals saved by their agility and their small size, survived the cataclysm. It only remained for the Earthmen to get to work.

But before this the Earthly astronauts had returned to their own planet to report what they had seen and what they had done. It was then that a learned professor from among

105

our ranks, who presided over the destinies of a unified world, thought of an audacious scheme.

The huge progress of our technique enabled us to have aims that were equally great: it was soon a question of raising upon Venus, from the animals which were there already and crossing them with human seed, a new race, endowed with the ability to think, which would be on its globe the equivalent of man on the Earth.

Thus, declared the scientist, we would avoid the obligation to keep on Venus a large number of people in the form of an expeditionary force. Our half-brothers on Venus. created after our pattern, would be quite capable of looking after their planet themselves, and getting the most out of the soil. All we would have to do would be to give them instructions until they were developed enough to run their planet without help. We would then proceed to exchange produce, and things grown on Venus would give great pleasure to Earthmen, who were beginning to get tired of the smallness and the monotony of their planet.

This suggestion aroused a wave of enthusiasm. All the newspapers upon the Earth, printed by invisible force fields, bore banner headlines MAN TO CREATE OTHER MEN. But the great man saw rise around him a circle of those who thought his ideas impossible.

'Master,' they said, 'we must take great care. Certainly we understand the satisfaction which we can all feel, and you first of all, for having succeeded in peopling a sphere which was doing no good to reasonable beings. But suppose these Venusians develop faster than you realise? Suppose they become very quickly as crafty as we are and even more so, they would soon take it into their heads to stand up to us, to treat us as colonialists, to throw us out, and, who knows, to invade in turn our good old planet Earth to take control of our goods and our resources? . . .'

The great master raised his head, reflected for a few minutes, and then replied, 'My good friends, if we always thought only of the possible inconvenience and harm that might arise from our successive discoveries and let these thoughts stop our progress we would still be in the stone age. Let us create these Venusians, this will be the greatest glory of humanity, man has raised in a part of this vast universe, living beings similar to himself: He has created Venusians in his own image.' (*Adam* in Hebrew, is to *adama* what *Earthman* is to *Earth* and *Venusian* to *Venus*.)

The dynamism of the great master brought the last hesitations to an end. Cheered by a delirious crowd, a fleet of space craft took off for Venus. There were specialists of all sorts on board, selected from every continent and placed in charge of one of the favoured followers of the master.

The first task that our technicians undertook was to modify the meterological conditions on Venus in order to make them more like those on her sister planet the Earth. The thick clouds which encircled the planets were condensed into rain; the water filled the deeper parts, making wonderful green oceans, however, the higher parts remained fertile continents. For the first time, when the rains ceased, the sun shone on Venus in the middle of a completely new sky, and the coastlines were lit up and reflected in the waters.

He whose idea the operation was, the favourite pupil of the master, received from his companions the nickname of Light Bearer, and which he bore for ever afterwards (In Latin, Lucifer.)

During the absence of the Earthmen the mammals which escaped the first cataclysm had bred in large numbers; and those which survived the recent deluge remained in sufficiently large numbers to permit the creation of new races. Artificial mutations, brought about thanks to the most recent discoveries of our biologists, began to give the most encouraging results, the stature of certain animals began to straighten to take on the vertical position and their skull cavities began to hold more and more advanced brains. Finally, the favourite pupil of the grand master was proud

107

to have given life to a new being, comparable to our great monkeys.

At this moment, having observed these monkeys and measured their ingenuity, our technicians once more began to have doubts on the success of their mission. 'Indeed,' they thought, 'are we not going to do a very foolish thing? Is not our creative act like sawing off the branch we are sitting on? How can we envisage even for a second raising a rival to ourselves? Who would think that the Venusians would remain our friends? . . .'

Worn with care, they sent a radio message to Earth thus: 'Consider last mutation undesirable—stop—advise annulling whole project—stopping all work awaiting new instructions.'

The reply came shortly afterwards in the form of a luxurious space craft of the cylindrical type which appeared one day in the skies of Venus and the master himself came out, followed by an escort of responsible people. An important conference was held, during which the master spoke in these terms:

'Gentlemen, you tend to exaggerate strongly the danger which the future Venusian could be—in our opinion. However wise they may become, centuries will have to pass before they could ever menace our safety; and we would have time to see them coming anyway.'

An imperceptible smile could be made out on the lips of several of his followers.

'Patron,' said the toughest of them, 'I am afraid that you are too good. You are judging the others like yourself. This will perhaps play you an unfortunate trick.'

The face of the wise man lit up with an indefinite expression and he replied:

'Trust me: I know what I am doing.'

As a result of this historic conference the followers of the great master divided into two camps holding opposing views: the one wishing to continue with the experiments and the others with Lucifer refusing to be responsible for any more. However, the day came when, despite the objections the master solemnly took out of a plastic case a small transparent tube in which human seed was enclosed. At the thought that he was going to inject this seed into one of the females of the most highly developed race, and from this female a hybrid being, half-Earthman, half-Venusian, would be born, the majority of our party were not able to conceal a shudder of disgust.

However, everything took place as the wise man had foreseen. After a reasonable lapse of time the planet Venus bore on its soil the first group of Venusians who had an appearance which was almost human, to whom it was possible to teach the rudiments of the terrestrian language. People wondered to see them going about their daily tasks, making tools to work with, and exchanging their impressions in which there were several abstract and several general ideas. . . .

'This is starting well,' murmured one of the 'light bearers', increasingly hostile to their patron's enterprise, as they thought they could foresee what, in their eyes, would be fatal for all of them if it happened. A day would come when the paternal help given by the terrestrian colonists would be intolerable to creatures endowed with their own willpower; they would raise a rebellion. Then there would be one of two things to do. Either massacre them to the last man or accept the fact of being ejected from the planet and leaving in outer space a Venus victorious, free, autonomous, and capable of anything—and of any sort of counter-attack. The idea of the invasion of the Earth by the liberated Venusians already began to spread among the members of the expeditionary force.

It was just at this moment when the wise man, having gathered the Venusians around him, spoke to them something like this:

'You have become reasonable beings and I believe that you can be relied upon. Henceforth you can do your own cooking yourselves, and you are each going to be given a small box of matches to light your fire. Needless to say I must tell you that it is absolutely forbidden and dangerous to use these matches for any other purpose.' The Venusians took the boxes that were given them and went away very contented.

The occasion was most successful and the faction of the pessimists lost ground.

From then onwards the Venusians received visits from certain Earthmen with determined foreheads, who gave them fascinating talks. Thus they learned that it was not true liberty to obey scrupulously the instructions given by the close followers of the great master; they would not be equals with man until they exercised their right of free choice; and to do some individual act that was unconventional which would be the sign of their future independence. The Venusians took this all in with great excitement.

The day came when the great master saw the door of his room burst open.

'Master, master,' cried one of his assistants, 'come and look, come quickly.'

Annoyed, because this intrusion had interrupted him during his weekly rest, the master went to the threshold and gave a cry: the sky was black with smoke, and huge flames were roaring up everywhere.

'Oh God!' cried the God of the Venusians. . . .

And he tried to find out what had happened.

'Oh almost nothing,' replied a voice. It was the man who had thought out the plan of rebellion, 'nothing that could not have been foreseen. Was it not you, master, who distributed the matches to all the Venusians? They have played with them and the fire has devoured their huts, then the flames reached their fields, then the savannaah, and they are not far from the forest. Soon all Venus will be burning.'

But it did not happen. The master hastened to the scene of the fire and gave rapid orders which ended in the fire being put out.

Most of the first Venusians perished in this catastrophe.

110

The survivors, most of them gravely disfigured, never completely recovered from the shock of their first and rough
meeting with evil; their descendants remain affected as a
result of this trouble.

The result of all this was that the 'light' group, denounced
by their unhappy victims, were punished by not being
allowed to return to Earth. Thus they remained on Venus
where they organised their own lives. To avoid being driven
out later by the Venusians they tried to reduce their intellect
and diminish their original faculties. They hoped to lower
themselves to the rank of monkeys and in many cases they
were completely successful.

CHAPTER TWELVE

The Sender and Those Sent

THIS HARMLESS fable shows us, as we have wished, the way that myths grew up in former times: accounts adorned by the simplest of images which tell of a reality which is very much more involved.

Let us note, in order to avoid all risk of being misunderstood, that we have at no time tried to identify the great master of our story with Him whom we call God the Father. For if tradition has not mislaid us, it is possible to imagine that there exists above us, an innumerable hierarchy of beings of which the psychic level is higher than ours and which occupy a scale of values which are quite above our comprehension. Between the 'best' of all and ourselves there exists an abyss in comparison with which, the space between a virus and a human being is only very small indeed.

Without running the risk of being contradicted, it can be supposed that every solar system obeys a living organisation composed of beings who are capable of the task, but they in their turn would be vassals of a superior race responsible to the galaxy, which in turn would be responsible to an intergalactic power, etc.

In this case the Supreme Being—if he exists—would occupy the summit of this universal pyramid or indeed (as it would be wiser to suppose) would he not exist outside this abundance of life in an impenetrable supernatural mystery?

But the reader may be reassured that we have no pretension here of trying to unravel the mystery of God.

However, it is certain, that in attributing to these intermediaries a certain number of activities which are usually thought to belong to the Almighty alone we are not committing any blasphemy: on the contrary, we are following in the wake of the most authentic traditions. If we continue to stress this point, it is to reassure any readers who are convinced Christians who might be shocked at any apparent departure from the Scriptures. There is nothing of fantasy in what we are saying and it can all be checked against the most reliable references.

The most fiercely monotheistic of all religions, that of the Jewish people, sees no contradiction between the belief in a single God, Yahveh, and a large number of messengers, who created a link between the great chief and ourselves, the inhabitants of the Earth. Furthermore, the editors of the Bible did not always distinguish very well between the Creator and his messengers; they freely confused the author of a message with the message sent by him. This confusion between the sender and the person sent is a very typical Hebrew failing. For example, the 'pillar of cloud' in the flight from Egypt, most often mentioned as a visible image of Yahveh, is also called, from time to time, the angel of Yahveh—the messenger of God. Abraham, who received the visit of the Lord, opened his eyes and saw three men coming towards him: and the 'angel of Yahveh' spoke to him as if he were God Himself. This way of writing, which offends our accurate minds, was still in use in the time when the New Testament was written, as these verses from the Revelation of St. John will show:

'And I, John, saw these things and heard them. And when I had heard and seen, I fell down and worshipped before the feet of the angel which showed me these things. Then saith he unto me, See thou do it not; for I am thy fellow

113

servant, and of thy brethren the prophets and of them which keep the sayings of this book: worship God.' And again: 'Behold I come quickly . . . I am Alpha and Omega, the beginning and the end, the first and the last. . . . I, Jesus, have sent my angel to testify unto you these things in the churches' (Revelation xxii, 8–16).

The angel spoke sometimes in his own name ('I am thy fellow servant') and sometimes in the name of Him who had sent him ('I Jesus, have sent my angel') without anything to mark where the change comes from the one person to the other.

Similarly, although the Biblical text several times declares that Moses talked with God himself on Sinai ('as one would speak to a friend') the fathers of the Church were not afraid to give this a much wider interpretation, and they believed, as in the case of the pillar of cloud, that Moses spoke merely to angels.

'These burning torches,' wrote St Hilary, 'these dazzling fires, these deafening thunderclaps, and the terror that accompanied the manifestation of God, betrayed the presence of angel messengers, who gave out the Law by means of a mediator [Moses].' In the Acts of the Apostles, written by the evangelist St Luke, Stephen, the first Christian martyr is heard declaring to his Jewish compatriots, '[You] who have received the law by the disposition of angels, and have not kept it' (Acts vii, 53). In the Epistle to the Hebrews, as in the Epistle to the Galatians, St Paul repeats that the law was promulgated by 'the angels', contrary to the new precepts received from the mouth of the Son of God himself. (Galatians iii, 19; Hebrews ii, 2–3.)

If it is feared that these New Testament texts tend to mislead deliberately the revelation of Moses in order to make the Gospels more convincing, here are other examples, which are purely of Judaic origin:

In the *Book of the Jubilees*, a Hebrew account, Yahveh is presented to us at the moment when he is entrusting the

114

editing and the publishing of the law to an 'angel', probably Michael, the angel of the Chosen People, called here 'the Angel of the Presance' and who, after Moses, interprets the commands of God. Similarly the Jewish historian Flavius Josephus, friend of the Romans, 'We have received from God, by the ministry of angels, the finest commands and the holiest of Laws.' These references, as well as the ones coming beforehand, are taken from the book by R. P. Daniélou, *Les Anges et leurs Missions*, published by Editions de Chèvetogne.

Thus it is not by wishful thinking to support our argument that we have removed the person of Yahveh from the heights of Sinai; other authors, who were authorities on the matter, have done it before us.

The importance of these conclusions will be evident when we have established that the contacts between the inhabitants of the Earth and the visitors from outer space were formerly much more frequent and confined to far fewer people than we dared to assume until now.

A very clear idea of the extent of these contacts can be obtained by reading a passage from the Bible which the scholars and theologians prefer to gloss over, because of its sensational and objectionable nature.

'The Sons of God saw the daughters of men that they were fair; and they took them wives of all which they chose. . . . There were giants [Nephilim] in the earth in those days; and also after that, when the sons of God came in unto the daughters of men, and they bear children unto them, the same became mighty men which were of old, men of renown.'

Yes, these are verses from the Old Testament, incorporated into Genesis vi, 2 and 4. The French Jerusalem Bible, in one of its notes, declares that this passage is 'difficult'. The theologians of the fourteenth century tried to explain away these embarrassing verses by declaring that the 'sons of God' were the descendants of Seth, the third son of Adam and Eve, and that the 'sons of men' were the descen-

115

dants of Cain—which did not explain why their marriages —completely human—should have brought forth giants. More in conformity with our ideas were the views of the early fathers who thought that the 'sons of God' meant 'angels', which, as we think, are creatures from outer space but in the main similar to us humans.

Is this allusion in the Bible the only instance where our theories are confirmed? Not in the least, as there are many instances of this in the folk lore of many countries. They tell in a poetic manner of similar cross-breeding of races.

The agreeable compliment paid by the authors of Holy Writ to those who passed on the Mediterranean myths will be noted: 'the same became the mighty men which were of old, men of renown'. One thinks at once of Herakles or Hercules, son of Zeus and Alcmena, an Earth woman; of the Minotaur, half man, half bull, son of Pasiphae and a mysterious 'white bull' which arose from the sea; of Castor, Pollux, and Perseus. . . .

But the shores of Greece and the Near East are not alone in the privilege of giving birth to this type of successful half-breed.

In much more recent times, the Inca monarchs, for example, whose origin is unknown to us (and who reigned over a people very different from us: the Quichua Indians), claimed to hold their authority and to derive their fine appearance from an origin outside the Earth—they claimed an ancestor named Manco Capac (*capac* meant 'chief' and is similar to the Latin *caput*), who had 'descended from the sky' to give laws to humans.

According to teachings called 'most secret' in old Tibet, the first ancestor of the Rlang family had come from above, 'after having crossed nine atmospheric layers', landing on a high mountain to make himself king among men. He was, it is said, accompanied by six little dwarfs (or beings short in stature), who could at will come down from the sky and go up there again. (Cf. *Au Tibet*, in *Naissance du Monde*, Editions du Seuil.)

Finally, the dynasty of the Japanese Emperors, according to a tradition still held today, was founded by Amaterasu, a being who rose out of the Sun.

Was there any reason that this 'Sun' from which these princes in search of kingdoms came down, was it any different from the 'Sun' which was seen dancing above Fatima or which so moved Pope Pius XII in the gardens of the Vatican?

If a spectacle of this nature was able to raise so much commotion among men of the twentieth century, the effect it would have on our forebears can only be imagined. It would give rise to a religious fear and they would greet the messengers with a mixture of reverence and eagerness as they had 'come down from the Sun'. These messengers would give them their laws, their beliefs, as well as their codes of morality; even better, they would teach them industrial techniques hitherto unknown until then.

The Gnostic manuscripts refer to the 'angel watchers', who, in order the better to seduce the 'daughters of men', would accompany their advances with gifts of precious stones (gold, silver), or useful metals (copper, iron), and which is quite touching, even placate the disappointed husbands by giving them advice on the way to found on our Earth the beginnings of an iron industry.

The *Book of Jubilees* and the *First Book of Enoch* apocryphal (that is to say, hidden) texts, contain similar information. But they present the instruction of the 'angels' (use of metals, art of writing, astronomy) as something evil which ought to bring punishment on them. (Cf. I Enoch, ch. 8.)

'And God saw that the wickedness of man was great in the earth and that every imagination of the thoughts of his heart was only evil continually. And it repented the Lord that he had made man on the earth and it grieved him at his heart. And the Lord said, I will destroy man whom I have created from the face of the earth; both man and beast, and

117

the creeping thing, and the fowls of the air; for it repenteth me that I have made them' (Genesis vi, 5–7).

And there was the Flood.

A manuscript in Coptic, discovered in a jar in 1945 (Cf. Jean Doresse, *Les Livres Secrets des Gnostiques d'Egypte*, Editions Plon) gives a very personal account of the event. If this account is to be believed the Hebrew tradition, that the Ark saved Noah and his family, is false. In reality Noah did not have to build a ship; accompanied by 'men of the perfect generation' (?) he found refuge in a luminous cloud, and remained there until the waters went down.

We are beginning to understand what is meant by these 'luminous clouds' which the Hindus also know under the name of Vimana. However, we scarcely like to give up, on the strength of one manuscript, the view commonly held, that the Ark was a real ship, especially as a Russian airman, during the First World War, declared that he saw a vessel of that nature, lying high and dry on the slopes of Mount Ararat in north-eastern Turkey.

CHAPTER THIRTEEN

The War on High

THE CURTAIN falls on this comedy of interplanetary morals in the form of a diluvian rain, which, in blotting out all terrestrial life, gives the world a new start. Everything was blotted out and life began again. A germ remained alive, destined to give the human race a new start.

But everything happens as if our destiny remained split between two contradictory tendencies, as if we were open at the same time to the influence of two hostile groups and as if our shepherds in space carried on a fierce struggle and in particular on our own doorstep.

We know only too well the stage at which a similar point of view conflicts with our modern way of thinking; the time is far off when people thought it natural to consider that 'good' and 'bad' angels existed, whose aims were mutually contradictory. (Let us note, after all, that this qualification of 'good' and 'bad' belongs only to one of the contending parties, and that the epithets would probably be reversed if the other side were using them. No one considers 'bad' the cause to which he devotes his whole body and mind, and all judgement of values depends on the point of view of the person giving it.)

Besides, when we mention only *two* opposing ways of thought, we underestimate very much the possible number of traditional teachings.

'What the "angels" were in charge of over whole nations' wrote St Basil in agreement with Origen, 'was the teaching of Moses and the Prophets.'

Let us add that they probably had a reliable source from which to make this statement. . . . Again, Clement of Alexandria said, 'God has given philosophy to the Greeks by means of inferior angels', and Origen declared that these same inferior angels gave the occult and secret sciences to the Egyptians, the astral religion to the Chaldeans and the promises of the Hindus concerning the 'science of God' (J. Daniélou, *Les Anges et leurs Missions*, op. cit.). This is also the opinion of certain contemporary scientists, among them the Soviet professor, Agrest.

It goes without saying that when the peoples had not only different interests, but also different methods of instruction, dissensions could not fail to come to light between their respective guardians. That is why an ancient Jewish prayer asked God 'to re-establish peace in the family above just as in the family below'.

But despite these divergences which were often purely local it is indeed *two* principal tendencies that we wish to take into account, of which one, usually, mobilises the majority of the forces available, while the other has only a minority, but a very aggressive minority.

We will give a generic and conventional name to the former, the 'natural forces' or 'Luciferians'; and the second we will call 'antinatural' or 'Yahvic'. Such a distinction necessitates that we pause here for a moment.

It is, indeed, impossible to understand our history properly unless the antagonism we have just mentioned is taken into account. Amidst the tangled skein of our lives on Earth it permits us to find a conductor rail thanks to which everything becomes increasingly understandable.

Let us say it once more: we are inventing nothing. It is essential that our reader is quite convinced of this. The only novelty brought into these pages is perhaps the way this thesis is presented, intentionally reduced to its simplest terms. Let us hope that this simplification will not draw upon the author the accusation that he has over-simplified the issue, and let us hope, too, that the reader will realise that there is a great difference between the outline theory given here and the complicated reality which it is supposed to represent.

The thesis, in itself, even if at times it runs contrary to conventional thought, has nothing revolutionary in it: it lacks it. But it seems to have been forgotten, or rather obliterated for the sake of a number of interests which are easy to imagine, and to the harm of a large number of our contemporaries who do not know on what criterion to base their attitude to life or the choice of what they do.

It is therefore useful to revive the thesis at a time when the advances of our science permit us to acclaim as possible or even probable a version of our history which only a short time ago would have been considered fantastic.

Natural law, set up on Earth with the appearance of Man, is a hard law. All evolution is linked by it to a merciless struggle. Life grows at the expense of other life. The strongest or the cleverest eat the weaker or the less astute. The balance of the terrestrial economy is, paradoxically, based on the fertility of decay; the finest roses grow on dung as an old proverb declared. All this, is, alas, only too well known.

And besides, although we realise that this is the order of things around us, we never succeed in resigning ourselves to it. The idea, for example, that the whole Earth is nothing more than a gigantic abattoir or that living things eat each other in order to survive offends our higher feelings and we prefer not to think of it as we cut our fillet of roast beef, our mutton, and especially when we swallow fresh oysters, still murmuring as a result of a drop of lemon. (If oysters

121

had eyes, as Gilbert Cesbron commented, would we dare lift them to our mouths?) The most delicate among us would like to prevent the massacre of animals and renounce feeding on their flesh.

But the cruelty of life most often leaves us bitter and spiteful. The evils which we see are not felt by us to be a necessary reality but as a practical joke or as an injustice.

The animal accepts his lot and behaves in the same way from generation to generation; our naturalists have discovered nothing to suppose that the worm, the frog, or even the chimpanzee consider condemning their circumstances as unfavourable and trying to improve them. Even the suicide of the scorpion, which is a very unusual case in zoological custom, does not seem to be an individual refusal to live, but corresponds to a rite inherent to the species, just like the sacrifice of the male praying mantis. All these instinctive laws are obeyed without any thought of avoiding them.

Man, in that, is quite different.

Imprisoned in a way of life which he finds unacceptable he does everything he can to get out of it. Anthropologists have noticed that the distinct human activity, in contrast to that of animals, is to try, by all means possible, to modify, subdue, and conquer that tyrannical nature against whom we are in open rebellion. Man is, above all things, a rebel. (On this subject cf. a remarkable study by Vercors in *Plus ou moins Homme*, edition Albin Michel.)

Why is this?

Doubtless this is because we are not at home on this Earth, and, at the bottom of our heart, we realise this.

We are, according to the Bible, 'strangers', 'travellers on Earth' (Psalm cxix, 19).

Perhaps we ought, indeed, as the ancient traditions affirm, to create a new order of things on our planet, taking the first step in reforming nature. Not destined to suffering, we are charged to cultivate our garden, that is to say to rearrange our domain according to our preferences and our tastes. 'Of every tree of the garden thou mayest freely eat', said Elohim of Genesis, and we know that the expression 'eat of the fruit of' was a Hebrew expression for 'experiencing' (eat the fruit of wisdom, eat the fruit of falsehood).

'But of the tree of knowledge of good and evil, thou shalt not eat of it': that is to say; 'do all the good you can with the exception of that which deviates from a certain imposed plan; if you do not you will soon learn to your cost what separates the good (what conforms to the plan) from the evil (what rises in opposition to the plan).'

In a fair way to becoming the rulers, we have allowed this supremacy to escape, doubtless as a result of the bad use to which our ancestors put their free will—perhaps under the influence of those who had an interest in depriving us of our privileges, in order to eliminate future competition: that is at least what is clearly shown in ancient reports. The famous 'revolt of the angels', which our fathers declared encompassed the skies, had man as its objective, one section of the extra-terrestrials having refused, one day, their duty of bowing the knee to the descendants of Adam. Once more we have invented nothing.

Fallen man found himself submitting to the laws of 'ancient nature', those which governed our globe before the advent of man. Our race became subject to usury, to illness, to death. Woman, grouped with female animals 'gave birth in pain'. Was this vengeance or punishment? Not at all, merely the simple and inescapable consequence of a return to the animal.

Those of us who are indignant at having to be subjected today to the consequences of an accident in which they were not personally involved, should think of the unfortunate people who were born deformed as a result of the radioactive fall-out at Hiroshima: were they responsible? Every catastrophe leads to repercussions which are only put right by the hand of time. . . .

Since that time everything has happened as if the forces of Lucifer had done their best to carry on down here the rule of the ancient 'nature', possessing the entire mastery of our globe. Has not Lucifer been called the 'Prince of this World'? In a Biblical passage (Ezekiel xxviii, 14) Yahveh spoke to Satan like this:

'Thou art the anointed cherub that covereth . . . thou wast upon the holy mountain of God. . . .'

The holy mountain: we understand that this meant the Earth, under the direction of the angel, before it became rebellious. 'This power . . . is delivered unto me', says Satan in the Gospel according to St Luke, and he can give it to anyone he likes. He is in his own home.

(Let us note in passing that Lucifer is shown to us as if he belonged to the Cherubim: we need wonder no more about the innumerable legends which describe 'devils' with cloven hoofs, we now know that 'demons' possess this trait in common with certain angels.)

On the contrary, the powers which we call 'Yahvic', from the name Yahveh of which they make use, are in open struggle against primitive 'nature'; they appear always to be animated by the desire to protect man. But the Earth is not their domain; their action is based from places outside, like commandos, as if our planet were for them enemy territory. Their intervention is sporadic and only limited in character.

We are not going to be long in discovering the main methods of their tactics, which are remarkable for their perseverance: the rescue operation to save our species operates in various stages, of which the first stage and that stage alone, covered almost twenty centuries. For it was about the year 1950 BEFORE Christ that the first action seems to have been taken by the Yahvists.

The stake was to oust the Luciferians from their hold on 'this world', and to deliver man from 'natural' laws by bringing about a change in his way of life.

124

CHAPTER FOURTEEN

The Adventure of a Citizen of Ur

IN THE twentieth century B.C. the situation on the terrestrial front seemed far from satisfactory to the Yahvist staff.

Under the domination of Lucifer, man seemed to be gradually getting used to the idea of integrating himself with 'nature', toiling for his living, fighting other men for the improvement of his own conditions of life. Finding compensation in the satiation of his low instincts, into which no moral question entered, he was quite right. It only remained for what was left of his spirit of revolt to disappear for nothing to differentiate him from the animals of the first creation.

In his relations with the beyond, always formidable, the cult of fertility, already described was accompanied by the use of the natural law of barter: giving and receiving. In order to obtain a favour from the gods, one made a sacrifice, an operation which consisted of giving up one good to obtain another. In this manner an advantage was obtained in exchange for a voluntary gift which should be as costly as possible.

This is why popular wisdom attributed the power of money to the Devil: every household when making its daily purchases, used without knowing it, the method of sacrifice.

When the chief riches of a people consisted in raising herds, a horned beast was sacrificed. But this was doubtless neither large nor generous enough. What therefore could a man sacrifice that was particularly dear to him if it were not a fellow-man, the image of himself? Human sacrifice was indeed the supreme form of sacrifice.

If the murder of one of our fellow-men, considered then as an act of great valour, seems to us completely abhorrent today, it is the result of progress made in the meantime by the Yahvist influence, resolutely opposed to such practices. 'To love his neighbour as himself is more than all whole burnt offerings and sacrifices,' proclaimed the good scribe to Jesus to the great scandal of the pagans (Mark xii, 33). We are for the most part become incapable of imagining the mentality of our ancestors, for whom the life of a human being was only officially worth the price which could be obtained for it.

Not only was the sacrifice of a man, a woman or a child a completely normal action and a meritorious one at that, but there were always eager volunteers who accepted death in order to give greater benefit to the community as a whole. Their companions did their best to make their end easier by the use of anaesthetics, after which the victims exposed their necks to the sword with a surprising amount of cheerfulness.

In India, just as among the Incas, the death of an important person was followed automatically by that of his wife and his servants. Spanish chroniclers of the conquest of the New World were witnesses of scenes of this nature, especially on the occasion of the death of Atahualpa. 'His wives gave themselves to the holocaust; they strangled themselves with their hair or threw themselves from the top of a rock.' Very often, owing to the large number of faithful servants who aspired to a similar fate, the reigning Inca had to intervene in order to moderate the ardour of the candidates for suicide. (Cf. Siegfried Huber, *Au Royaume des Incas*, Editions Plon.)

In Chaldea, recent excavations made by French archaeologists have brought to light skeletons of children

126

sealed between stones which served as foundations of dwelling-places: they played the role of bringer of good luck. Read this quotation from the Bible (I Kings xvi, 34): 'In his days did Hiel the Bethelite rebuild Jericho [destroyed by Joshua's troops] he laid the foundations thereof in Abiram his first-born, and set up the gates thereof in his youngest son Segub.' It is hardly likely that this Hiel of Bethel acted in this way out of gaiety of spirit but with the feeling of doing a duty and to give a good example.

In a similar manner complete charnel-houses have been found containing the remains of men, women and children which is enough to supply vivid evidence for the point we are making. (Cf. *Histoire Sainte*, by Daniel-Rops, *La Bible arrachée aux Sables*, by W. Keller and *Light on the Bible*, by the British archaeologist James B. Pritchard.)

In other countries where the religious spirit was tempered to a certain extent things that were loved were not sacrificed: they were replaced by prisoners seized from some enemy, and the Aztec kings waged war especially to obtain this precious 'game' to be sacrificed on their altar. And in the places where the cult of the god was no longer completely sincere, such as in the later Roman period, these massacres were retained as part of the public games and to serve as a distraction for the crowd.

It is perhaps not out of place to note that if these practices have disappeared in theory, if they have more or less ceased playing a large part in public life, they have not finished their ravages. According to what is known today of the secret beliefs of Adolf Hitler, it is permissible to wonder if the systematic sacrifice of six million Jews, carried out under racial pretexts, and also in the excuse of serving certain political interests, was not a gigantic sacrifice in order to gain certain favours. The Luciferians had good reason to be anti-Semite: it is easy to understand why.

This was the current atmosphere in these 1950 years before

Christ; if one adds all that has already been told in these pages concerning the lascivious cults of Baal, one cannot help thinking that it must have been a depressing enough atmosphere for the extra-terrestrial supporters of Yahvism, who, nevertheless, had decided to pursue their objectives.

In the city of Ur, in Chaldea, there lived a man whose name, in the language of the time, meant, 'he whose father is great', for he came from an important family. The fact that he had no children had absolved him from the necessity of sacrificing one of them to the success of his concerns; he lived surrounded by a numerous household of women, brothers, nephews, nieces, servants, and everyone worshipped the local Baal with a clear conscience. Besides, our Akkadian benefited, as an educated man, from the instruction given by the messengers from outer space to his countrymen—instruction which did not separate the movement of the stars from their connection with terrestrial happenings; there was no pure astronomy in those far-off times, it was always confused with astrology.

It was no doubt his knowledge of heavenly bodies that caused this man to be noticed by the Yahvist general staff: because their project needed the participation of such a man as he. Messengers were sent to him who did not apparently belong to the family of the Cherubim, although they worked in close liaison with them. But their nature must have been completely different as they appeared as young men in the prime of life, although somewhat stylised. As for knowing whether these beings had taken on that particular form temporarily or whether it was their real appearance (which supposes the existence of a human race like ours, which is difficult to believe), or yet—and this theory is worth remembering, we shall see why—perhaps they were men like you or me but passed over to the Yahvist cause long ago and 'sublimated' as was Elijah many years later, can only remain in the field of conjecture.

Let us recall that during the recent wave of flying saucer

128

sightings witnesses have declared that they have seen in the vicinity of these craft not only dwarfs covered in space suits but men. If these men exist, could they be of the same race as are mentioned in the sacred texts? This would seem to be good to be true, but where in this field do we know where are the limits of possibility?

Let us leave this point and return to our Akkadian, who was receiving three 'men' who declared they were envoys from Heaven and who was greeting them with the welcome they deserved.

The three men ordered him to leave Ur, the great city, and by this act to show his complete break with the contemporary world. The Akkadian obeyed, he left, with all his things, to settle in the provinces, in Haran, a very small town. But this was not enough, the former citizen, under instruction from his mysterious counsellors, left his sedentary habits there to take on the nomadic life, taking with him in the new existence his wife, his nephews, his servants and his flocks.

There, when he was camping in the neighbourhood of the oak of Mamre the three emissaries rejoined him and told him that one day he would be given a posterity as numerous as the sands of the sea; that his name Abram (the man with a great father) would be changed to Abraham (the father of many). And the visible sign of this agreement was, as night fell, the passage of an object like a 'whirlwind of smoke' and a 'torch of fire' which flew over the animals offered in ritual sacrifice. Another version describes the objects as a 'smoking furnace and a burning lamp'. But the word 'whirlwind' suits us better as it can serve equally to describe the 'flying chariot' which took Elijah up to heaven.

But Abram was old and his wife sterile; and the announcement of her coming baby took on something of the burlesque in the eyes of his wife and she laughed aloud in the presence of the envoys—who were busily eating the excellent roast veal (cf. Genesis xviii. 7-8) specially prepared for the occasion.

129

The meal over, the young men asked Abraham to show them the way which led to Sodom and Gomorrha; his nephew Lot lived in Sodom. It was just at this crucial moment that the two cities were destroyed, which Abraham saw from afar, having obtained grace for Lot 'and lo, the smoke of the country went up as the smoke of a furnace.'

Two Luciferian capitals had just been volatilised. Abraham was going to have a son; the first page of history had turned.

In fact, Abraham had two sons. The first, Ishmael, born of a servant of his wife, was driven out on the order of Sarah, and nearly died of hunger in the desert; saved by an 'angel', he is generally considered to be the ancestor of the Moslem world.

As for Yshq, the child of laughter—as the name means, anglicised to Isaac, the child Sarah bore contrary to all expectations, she had long passed the age of child-bearing, there is no need to retell here how Abraham did not sacrifice him according to the rites of Ur, or how a last-minute intervention, in the best style of the thriller novel, preserved him for his destiny.

Isaac (Yshq) was the father of Jacob, surnamed Israel 'he who has power with god': Jacob, indeed had had the chance, one evening, to enter into a struggle against an 'angel' had not been defeated. He came out of the struggle with a slight sprain on the hip.

Jacob had twelve sons, from whom sprang the twelve tribes of the Jewish people: a people who were not 'elected' but created by selection. The Yahvic plan was following its course.

Just as it had been necessary to withdraw Abram from the surroundings of the city of Ur to separate him from the world of Lucifer, for the same reason his descendants had

130

to be brought out of the zone of influence of the Pharaohs of Egypt.

The little people were ripe for autonomy. The time had come to give them a code, a 'law,' which, in counteracting the effects of the former 'nature' would gradually give them a new point of view. It is difficult for us to imagine at what point this law would seem inhuman to the companions of Moses.

While the Luciferian rites incited people to sacrifice, Moses, passing on the instruction he had received, declared 'Thou shalt not kill'. And as for the victim of the sacrifice, in the new order man had to leave that to an animal, and, what is more, the law specified what animals should be selected.

While the Baals encourage the ravishing of women, raising the orgy to the level of a religious practice Moses said 'Thou shalt not commit fornication'. The establishment of chastity to the list of moral necessities must have at that time seemed absolutely incomprehensible and revolutionary; and unique besides. For this people coming from Akkadia and penetrating the learning of the Egyptians, the announcement of this commandment would be like a thunderclap. And besides, accustomed as we are in the west to see religions accompanied by restrictions of this nature, we have not yet succeeded in understanding clearly the reason for it.

Indeed, as well as the commandments which repressed lying and stealing, and whose novelty was not altogether stupefying, Moses imposed on his followers the exclusive adoration of one God, Yahveh—a God humans could not imagine, and Who could not be portrayed in mosaics, silver, or gold, a God Whom no one could look at in the face and live. Here again the law offended the mental outlook of the people, as every god had a statue erected to him, which in some way was transformed into the god himself. As for worshipping one God only, that would assuredly mean turning one's back on all other gods, and the ancients were particularly well placed to realise that in fact they arose everywhere, especially on the Sun. . . .

It must always be borne in mind that the Law of Moses was a great shock to his people. Tacitus wrote along these lines much later; 'Moses gave [to these people] rites that were new and in strong contrast to those of other people. What was profane to them is sacred with us and what is allowed with them is profane to us'. (Quoted by Robert Aaron in *Les Années Obscures de Jésus,* published by Grasset).

There is nothing surprising that the inauguration of this anti-natural law needed a spectacular phenomenon to impress it on the people, the landing of the mother-ship on the heights of Sinaï. Little less would force the Hebrew people, impressed by the wonder, to accept such restrictions. But even then they did not accept them without a protest, despite the punishment which was immediately inflicted and which led to the death of a large number of rebels.

Was not the descent on Sinaï merely the landing of a flying 'cigar' which had occurred already several times? Had not the escape from Egypt been effected as a result of a series of plagues from which the Hebrews were miraculously immune? Had not the Red Sea, or Reed Sea, been parted to help the fleeing Israelites, only to fall back on their pursuers? Had not a nourishing manna fallen from the sky to keep the people vigorous in the desert?

The verse of Exodus xiv. 21 mentions a strong wind from the East which God caused to blow all night which dried up the sea. Modern commentators, anxious to interpret all these details by natural causes have thrown themselves on that verse in their attempts to explain away the miracle as caused by a strong wind; and the 'sea' for them, has been reduced to a mere marsh. But how then could there have been walls of water on each side between which the Hebrew people marched—'and the waters were a wall unto them on their right hand and on their left'. If it be true that our visitors possess the ability which enables them to bring into play force fields capable of thwarting the power of gravity the separation of water between two vertical walls would be easy for them. In the same way it would be easy for them to put a drag on the wheels of the Egyptian chariots, which advanced very slowly and with difficulty before the waters returned and engulfed them.

The manna, too, has found very varied natural explanations. It is said that it is a result of the resin secreted by the tamarisk when holes are made by ladybirds; others declare that manna is a species of lichen something of a cross between an onion and seaweed, whose nutritive value is very high and is almost as high as that of the chlorella.... Nevertheless, if such food was found in the deserts as has been made out, one wonders why the Hebrews, learning from the accounts of the numerous caravans which crossed the sands at that time, took this manna to be celestial food. We think that it is more similar to the 'whitening grains of seed' which dissolve in the heat of the day, to similar objects which fell as rain at Fatima, and when several other unidentified objects flew over. Doubtless these had no value as food but disintegrated also under the heat of the rays of the Sun.

The necessity to create a dramatic atmosphere when the laws were given that would create a lasting impression in the minds of the Hebrews was openly expressed in the Bible: 'And the Lord said unto Moses, Lo, I come unto thee in a thick cloud that the people may hear when I speak with thee, and believe thee for ever'.

No one could ever make a franker statement.

What did it matter if among the people there were a certain number of thick-headed, stiff-necked people who distorted the law or abandoned it for the practices common among the surrounding nations? 'I have kept unto myself seven thousands souls who have not bowed the knee to Baal,'

133

FLYING SAUCERS THROUGH THE AGES

declared Yahveh to Elijah. The performance of this elite, unsullied by any alliance with outside peoples or by other faiths was enough for the accomplishment of the Yahvic purpose.

We are passing over the vicissitudes of the Hebrews, their establishment in the land of Canaan, their internal and external problems, their victories, their defeats, their deportations, their returns from exile. It is important, however, not to lose sight of the conductor rail which runs through these inevitable events without interruption.

A thousand years—slightly less—separate Abraham from the reign of David. Another thousand years—almost exactly —were to pass by before a Jewish couple, descended from this same David, gave birth to a daughter, for whose creation the Yahvists had worked for twenty centuries, that faultless marvel, produced from a completely pure race, without any of the shortcomings inherent in ancient 'nature'.

This is, literally, in the Roman Catholic tradition, the meaning of the words immaculate conception, which a badly informed public tends to mistake with virginity. By the dogma of the immaculate conception the Roman Catholic church declares merely that Mary was of pure birth, that is to say purified from the consequences of original sin.

Myriam, herself the future mother of Yoshua, whose name, borrowed from Joshua, the immediate successor of Moses, means 'he who saves'.

Myriam, announced by Isiah seven centuries earlier: 'Therefore the Lord himself shall give you a sign; Behold a virgin shall conceive and bear a son and shall call his name Emmanuel' (God in our midst. Isiah vii. 4.)

'And ... the Angel Gabriel was sent from God unto a city of Galilee, named Nazareth, to a virgin espoused to a man whose name was Joseph ... and the virgin's name was Myriam. And the angel came unto her and said Hail, thou that art highly favoured, the Lord is with thee: blessed art thou among women. And when she saw him, she was troubled at his saying, and cast in her mind what manner of salutation this should be. And the Angel said unto her, Fear not, Myriam, for thou hast found favour with God. And behold, thou shalt conceive in thy womb, and bring forth a son, and shall call his name Yoshua. He shall be great and shall be called the son of the highest.... Then said Myriam unto the angel, How shall this be, seeing that I know not a man? And the Angel answered and said unto her, The Holy Ghost shall come upon thee, and the power of the Highest shall overshadow thee: therefore also that holy thing which shall be born of thee shall be called the Son of God.... And Myriam said, Behold the handmaid of the Lord; be it unto me according to thy word. And the Angel departed from her.' (St Luke i. 26-38).

If we have used the Hebrew names of Myriam and Yoshua instead of their usual translations, Mary and Jesus, it is to avoid the customary reaction of the reader to something that he has known for a very long time.

CHAPTER FIFTEEN

The Kingdom Which is Not of This World

WE HAVE at our disposal four gospels, according to Matthew, Mark, Luke and John: there is no reason to alter a syllable of them to find agreement with what we have already said. On the contrary, a number of verses which up till now contained obscurities suddenly become intelligible in the new light.

It is enough to read them again. But will it not be as if we are reading them for the first time? . . .

Our imaginations have given us various images of Jesus: for some He is a wise man, enemy of violence, defender of the poor, preaching peace in the midsts of a hostile world; for others He is a false prophet, seductor of crowds, founder of a sect; for yet other people He is an initiate comparable with Zoroaster, Buddha and Mahomet; philosopher and moralist; wonder-worker, creator of remarkable phenomena fakir; illusionist; or even the son of God, the incarnation of the word, and the second person of the Trinity. . . .

Among the current errors, let us note those which think that the characteristic traits of Jesus of Nazareth, those which distinguished Him from the ordinary run of men, resided in His ability to work miracles or in the originality of the way of life He taught. Yet, we have seen how others beside Him have been able to cure the sick, to walk upon the waters, to increase bread, especially certain prophets of His race. Others besides Him have preached the love of one's neighbour, and if no one has ever preached as well as Him, there is not, nevertheless a complete originality about his sermons.

On the other hand, several things had never been said before His day such as: 'My kingdom is not of this world,' and this other: 'Now shall the prince of this world be cast out. And I, if I be lifted up from the earth, will draw all men unto me' (John xii, 31–32).

This prediction brings us back into the sphere of that war between Yahvists and Luciferians, of which the history of Jesus seems to be a culminating episode. Let us take one by one all the verses which give Christ's point of view: we will find the affirmation repeated many times of an implacable hostility towards what we have called here the 'ancient nature', the condemnation in definite terms of that economy which causes 'necessary evil'. 'It is necessary that there be evil,' said Jesus, 'but woe unto him who causes it.'

And this statement recalls another one, which promises to the disciples of Christ a liberation from this nature: 'He who follows Me will never see death.' Every expression of His thought lights up his character as reformer come to abolish the 'natural' way of life, in the midst of which man struggles, and to replace it by another way of life, in the midst of which mankind would enjoy a happier fate, more in conformity with his true vocation.

It will be enough to re-read the Bible. . . .

Compare, for example, Luke iv, 5–8: 'And the devil, taking him up to a high mountain, showed unto him all the kingdoms of the world in a moment of time. And the devil said unto him, All this power will I give thee, and the glory of them: for that is delivered unto me; and to whomsoever

I will I give it. If thou therefore wilt worship me, all shalt be thine. And Jesus answered and said unto him, Get thee behind me, Satan: for it is written, Thou shalt worship the Lord the God and him only shalt thou serve.'

Or take Luke x, 17: 'And the seventy returned again with joy, saying, Lord, even the devils are subject unto us through thy name.'

Or John xvi, 11 and 13: '. . . the prince of this world is judged . . . but be of good cheer, I have overcome the world.'

Other parts of the New Testament will undergo a similar change before our eyes.

We have already mentioned the descent of a luminous cloud in the valley which dominated Bethlehem at the moment the birth of Jesus was announced to the shepherds. We have also mentioned the star which went before the Magi and which stopped above the house where the Infant was lying. Here are other glimpses of the Beyond in the life of the Nazarean:

'Now, when all the people were baptized, it came to pass, that Jesus also being baptized and praying, the heaven was opened, And the Holy Ghost descended in a bodily shape like a dove upon him . . .' (Luke iii, 21–22).

Jesus 'took Peter and John and James, and went up into a mountain to pray. And as he prayed, the fashion of his countenance was altered, and his raiment was white and glistening. And, behold, there talked with him two men, which were Moses and Elias; who appeared in glory, and spake of his decease which he should accomplish at Jerusalem. But Peter and they that were with him were heavy with sleep: and when they were awake, they saw his glory, and the two men that stood with him. And it came to pass as they departed from him, Peter said unto Jesus, Master, it is good for us to be here; and let us make three tabernacles; one for thee, and one for Moses, and one for Elias: not knowing what he said. While he thus spake, there came

138

a cloud, and overshadowed them: and they feared as they entered into the cloud. And there came a voice out of the cloud, saying, This is my beloved Son: hear him.' 'And when the disciples heard it, they fell on their face, and were sore afraid, And Jesus came and touched them and said, Arise, and be not afraid. And when they had lifted up their eyes, they saw no man, save Jesus only. And as they came down from the mountain, Jesus charged them, saying, Tell the vision to no man until the Son of Man be risen again from the dead' 'And they kept it close, and told not man in those days any of those things which they had seen.' (A combination of the synoptic accounts according to Luke ix, 28–36 and Matthew, xvii, 6–9.)

Even if the meaning of the feasts in the liturgical year has no meaning at all to the majority of our contemporaries, everyone knows that the spring brings in the bells of Easter and that on that day Christians commemorate the Resurrection of their Saviour. To those whose faith is particularly strong, the Resurrection is an event of supreme importance, without which the life of Jesus loses all its meaning. As St Paul wrote to the Christians of Corinth: 'If Christ be not raised, then is our preaching vain, and your faith is also vain' (I Cor. xv, 14).

For all other men, this Resurrection did not take place, was not able to take place, for the good reason that the laws of nature being what they are a resurrection—that is to say a return from death to life—is impossible.

We must stress the phrase 'the laws of nature being what they are', because a certain number of things, 'impossible' in certain defined conditions, could become 'possible' in the sphere of different natural laws. That natural laws different from what we consider to be normal can exist is beginning to be admitted by modern physicians as a result of recent experiences, which forces them to take such ideas seriously.

To take an example: in order to solve the mystery of anti-particles (positrons, anti-protons, anti-neutrons), the American physician Feynmann was not afraid to suggest that perhaps they were grains of matter living in reverse time, this is, going from the future to the past. Although such a theory is almost impossible for the human mind to visualise, it can be worked out quite satisfactorily in mathematics. Another physician, the Swiss Stückelberg (Cf. Jacques Bergier, *les Murailles Invisibles*, Edition Del Duca), has gone as far as supposing that there exists outside our perception a universe composed entirely of the anti-matter, whose particles stray dangerously near us.... Of course, these examples have no direct bearing on the case with which we are concerned: we merely cite them in order to remind the reader that everything has not been discovered yet and that our suggestion regarding the existence of a natural law different from what we are normally accustomed to is not pure phantasy. It is not only possible, in the eyes of science it is becoming more and more probable.

There is nothing that permits us to say from our own experience, which is of necessity bound to a certain set of natural laws, that this or that could not happen under a different set of rules of which we know nothing.

We have heard biological mutations mentioned; we know that they consist of the appearance of a new characteristic which alters the make-up of the species concerned. This characteristic is carried on by the normal method of hereditary and the new characteristic becomes normal in the new species thus created. But before a mutation takes place, the modification which is the result does not yet exist in nature, a study of the species up till then would assume its non-existence, its impossibility. Thus, at the time when the Earth was populated only by fish and reptiles, the existence of a fox-terrier or that of a giraffe would be impossible, as the conditions which made them possible would not yet have occurred.

If a dead person one day came to life again before our

eyes, that would not mean that our knowledge of biology was faulty, that this resurrection was possible, even though we did not know this: it would mean rather that on this occasion something new had happened, and as a result, something that was previously impossible could now take place. These are the new facts which make mutations possible.

Now it was indeed a mutation that the Yahvist entities were, it seems, trying to produce in the womb of the human species, according to a plan put into execution at the time of Abraham of Ur. Two thousand years had been devoted to bring together the conditions necessary for its production, two thousand years of careful selection, marriages planned according to a careful genetic scheme, two thousand years of preparation which was psychological as well as physiological; two thousand years of persistence in selecting the ancestors of a woman sufficiently perfect to conceive in her turn—according to standards which remain unknown to us—a 'son' whose nature was changed and not completely terrestrian, which would be shown by the continuance of His life after a temporary death.

Thus, what had been impossible up to that time became possible.

Thus at the same time a continuous and coherent link is revealed between events scattered all down history and whose connection had not been clear until now. The destiny of the line of Abraham, culminating in the 'Resurrection' of Jesus gives meaning to a whole series of events hitherto unconnected. (Sense and direction at the same time.)

In the midst of the stagnation of the ancient peoples, who developed merely to disperse in death, a current of living history flows, which rises at Ur, and flows like a river whose waters do not mix with those of the lakes they pass through.

The existence and permanence of the Jewish people among the pagan nations with completely different morals remains an insoluble mystery which all historians have failed to solve. Deprived of this essential reason for exist-

141

ence, the history of this group of people defies all explanation: if it were not true, it would be most unlikely.

On the other hand, if we accept the theory of this purpose, if the foundation of the people of Israel had for an objective the production of a new type of 'Earthman' (St Paul called Jesus 'the new Adam'), freed from the servitude of 'ancient nature' we suddenly understand what had previously been a mystery.

Why should we refuse to accept a logical solution when it presents itself, which is a great advantage over the absurd and the arbitrary?

'The first day of the week cometh Mary Magdalene early, when it was yet dark, unto the sepulchre, and seeth the stone taken away from the sepulchre. Then she runneth, and cometh to Simon Peter, and to the other disciple, whom Jesus loved, and saith unto them, They have taken away the Lord out of the sepulchre, and we know not where they have laid him. Peter therefore went forth, and that other disciple, and came to the sepulchre. So they ran both together: and the other disciple did outrun Peter, and came first to the sepulchre. And he, stooping down, and looking in, saw the linen clothes lying, yet went he not in. Then cometh Simon Peter, following him, and went into the sepulchre, and seeth the linen clothes lie, And the napkin that was about his head, not lying with the linen clothes, but wrapped together in a place by itself. Then went in also that other disciple, which came first unto the sepulchre, and he saw, and believed. For as yet they knew not the scripture, that he must rise again from the dead' (John xx, 1–9).

Compare this with the psalm of David, xvi, 9–11: 'Therefore my heart is glad, and my glory rejoiceth: my flesh also shall rest in hope. For thou wilt not leave my soul in hell: neither wilt thou suffer thine Holy One to see corruption. Thou wilt show me the path of life: in thy presence is ful-

ness of joy; at thy right hand are pleasures for evermore.'
(Probably written nine or ten centuries before Christ.)

The new Adam, the mutated Man, the Yahvist Man, had
just been born. Thence forward by right if not in fact, the
human race—in the person of one of its members—had
found its true destination. One man, among all, had
escaped the natural law of death and of corruption, thus
opening to all other men 'of good will', the road to survival.

The domination of Lucifer, for the first time, suffered a
mortal blow: the walls of its fortress had begun to crumble
away at one point and it only remained for its attackers to
enlarge the breach. 'The day approacheth,' said Jesus, 'when
the Prince of this world shall be overthrown.'

Everything to do with Christ gives rise to ready-made ideas,
generally without basis, but imposed by custom. We will not
be surprised if some people, when they read of our comparison of the life of Jesus with a 'biological mutation', feel
a sort of embarrassment, if we had, in doing so, committed
some sort of incongruity, or even had made fun of a subject
which deserved an attitude of respect. Such a sentiment
could be felt as much by unbelievers as by believers. We do
not think it superfluous to state once more that our assertions are neither irreverent or even very original.

We agree that the word 'mutation' has not often been
used to describe the existence of Christ. But the idea behind
these expressions is not in the least new. It can be found all
down the ages of Christianity. It can be found, differently
worded in several passages of the epistles of St Paul, all of
which are inspired writings.

The apostle, of course, used the language of his time and
not that of modern biologists. But he said of Jesus that His
victory over death made Him the 'New Man', the 'New
Adam', the fruit of a 'New Creation', the first of our race to
have been set free from the 'Ancient Law'.

The 'New Adam', that is to say, etymologically, the new

Earthman, shorn of his former restrictions, freed from his 'body of death' (another Pauline expression), in opposition to the 'old man', enslaved in his miserable condition since the fall of Adam in Genesis, the first man.

The Jewish Talmud, reflecting the oral traditions whose origins came from Moses, expresses the same idea when it declared that the coming of the Messiah would bring 'not only a physical and material transformation, but an evolution. The personality of the Messiah would be the culmination of a physical process in the nature of Man and in the power of the Universe' (H. Serouya, *La Kabbale*, Editions Grasset). A transformation, which, for the believing Jews would not become effective until it spread to all the good, in the day which they called 'The day of the Lord', and the Christians 'The Second Coming', or 'The Resurrection of the Flesh'.

As St Paul wrote to the Christian at Rome: 'For they that are after the things of the flesh despise the things of the flesh [i.e. natural law], but they that are after the [Yahvist] Spirit, the things of the Spirit. For to be carnally minded is death; but to be spiritually minded is life and peace. Because the carnal mind is enmity against God: for it is not subject to the law of God, neither indeed can be' (Romans viii, 5–7).

'For we know that the whole nation groaneth and travaileth in pain together until now. And not only they, but ourselves also, which have the first-fruits of the [Yahvist] Spirit, even we ourselves groan within ourselves, waiting for the redemption, to wit, the redemption of our body' (Romans viii, 22–23).

'For I reckon that the sufferings of this present time are not worthy to be compared with the glory which shall be revealed in us. For the earnest expectation of the creature waiteth for the manifestation of the sons of God' (Romans viii, 18–19).

Thus far from deserving the accusation of being a daring innovator, we lay ourselves open to the reverse accusation:

of falling dully into a retrograde conformity. Are we revolutionary or traditionalist? It is for the reader to decide.

The term 'mutated man' when given to Jesus, in reality raises another problem. We have seen that there enters into the biological definition of a mutation the passing on of the new characteristic to succeeding generations; without which the new characteristic can only be called a passing anomaly. Now as for the New Man, Christ did not pass His nature on to anyone.

There is a very sensible objection, which makes it necessary for us to go into our theory in more detail. Although Jesus Christ did not leave His gifts to an Earthly posterity, nevertheless St. Paul several times uses the word 'heritage' and describes his Christian brothers as heirs, at least heirs-presumptive.

Now Jesus said: 'That which is born of the flesh is flesh; that which is born of the spirit is spirit [. . . .] No one can see the Kingdom of God without being born on high.' Mysterious words which do not seem to have been understood by the person, Nicodemus, to whom they were addressed; and we must admit that we are all, to a greater or lesser extent, like Nicodemus when we try to understand these verses.

Prisoners of the 'ancient nature' we have no choice of methods of being born and of procreation, and what we have always known seemed hitherto to be satisfactory. But if we believe in Jesus this will no longer be our lot if we take on one day the 'Yahvist nature'.

'And Jesus . . . said unto them, The children of this world marry and are given in marriage: But they which shall be accounted worthy to obtain that world, and the resurrection from the dead, neither marry or are given in marriage: Neither can they die any more: for they are equal to the angels' (Luke xx, 34–36).

This future is perhaps not altogether rosy for us, fond as we are of certain advantages inherent in our 'ancient

145

nature', advantages that we would be saddened to give up. We know what we shall lose; but we do not know what we shall gain in such a transformation of our being.

But nature as we know it gives us examples of many different methods of reproduction, by division, by spores, by budding, by connection, and by sexual intercourse proper. . . . How could we define the attitude of an amoeba, accustomed to reproduce by simply dividing into two, which became sad at the idea of having to give up a method so simple for a superior method which it could not imagine?. . . The Universe is large enough to have many surprises in store for us. We gladly quote for the reader the savoury page from *Miracles* (Geoffrey Bles), which we owe to the late C. S. Lewis, a British theologian of Magdalen College, Oxford, who knew how to combine the highest philosophical thoughts with a sharp sense of British humour:

'The letter and spirit of scripture, and of all Christianity, forbid us to suppose that life in the New Creation will be a sexual life; and this reduces our imagination to the withering alternative either of bodies which are hardly recognisable as human bodies at all or else of a perpetual fast. As regards the fast, I think our present outlook might be like that of a small boy, who, on being told that the sexual act was the highest bodily pleasure should immediately ask whether you ate chocolates at the same time. On receiving the answer 'No', he might regard absence of chocolates as the chief characteristic of sexuality. In vain would you tell him that the reason why lovers in their carnal raptitudes do not bother about chocolates is that they have something better to think of. The boy knows chocolate; he does not know the positive thing that excludes it. We are in the same position. We know the sexual life; we do not know, except in glimpses, the other thing, which, in Heaven, will leave no room for it. Hence where fulness awaits us we anticipate fasting.'

These reflections lead us to wonder if there is not, according to the expression of the evangelists, a birth of the spirit, an allusion to a method of reproduction by the man after mutation. Tradition is not opposed to the idea of reproduction by the projection by the mind of the self outside itself, a real method of reproduction which is superior and according to which our theologians were able to say that Christ was really the Son of God. . . . In this way, Jesus, risen again, really did transmit a new life to all those who accepted regeneration by him.

Similarly we can assume that the majority of the phenomena called paranormal, connected with mysticism (such as levitation, radiation, the sudden transference from one place to another, the quick replacement of organic tissues, the multiplication of food, etc.) were really sporadic intrusions of the new nature in place of the old—and in all cases these caused a great stir in the districts where they occurred. There is much to say on this subject, but we are entering there into a region of pure speculation, whose snares up till now we have been able to avoid. Let us limit ourselves therefore to noting what is clearly shown in our ancient texts, too often badly read, too often distorted by our prejudging them.

After leaving the tomb, Jesus appeared alive to His disciples on several occasions and in various places. He spoke, He ate food, He let Himself be touched. He bore the marks of the blows He had received, and the marks of the nails. Nevertheless He had changed in appearance there was something indefinable that made Him different from His former Self. Doors did not have to be opened before He could come into a room full of people, and He disappeared suddenly without anyone seeing Him go. He was seen here, then there, and sometimes it took people several minutes to recognise Him.

One day, surrounded by His disciples, He reproached

them for their obstinacy and that of those who would not believe that He was alive. 'They asked in their defence: Master, this world of iniquity and unbelief is under the domination of Satan, who does not allow those who are under the yoke of the impure spirits to receive the Truth and the Power of God. But reveal thy justice to us now. Christ replied unto them, The end of the years of Satan's power are at hand, and however, other terrible things are at hand.' This little-known passage occurs in a manuscript of the Gospel according to St. Mark. (Quoted in a note to Mark xvi, 9 in the French Jerusalem Bible.)

The disciples 'asked of him, saying, Lord, wilt thou at this time restore the kingdom to Israel? And he said unto them, it is not for you to know the times or the seasons, which the Father hath put in his own power.' 'But of that day and hour knoweth no man, no, not the angels of heaven, but my Father only.' 'But ye shall receive power, after that the Holy Ghost is come upon you: and ye shall be witnesses unto me both in Jerusalem and Judaea and in Samaria, and unto the uttermost part of the earth. And when he had spoken these things, while they beheld, he was taken up; and a cloud received him out of their sight. And while they looked steadfastly towards heaven as he went up, behold, two men stood in white apparel; Which also said, Ye men of Galilee, why stand ye gazing up into heaven? this same Jesus, which is taken from you into heaven, shall so come in like manner as ye have seen him go to heaven. Then returned they unto Jerusalem from the mount called Olivet, which is from Jerusalem a sabbath day's journey.' (Acts i, 6–12 and Matthew xxiv, 36.)

The word power is from the Greek *dynamis*, which is often translated today as 'energy', 'force', or by the ancient term 'virtue'.

We possess other accounts of the Ascension which are not found among the canonical texts, such as those in the *Apocryphon Jacobi* and the *Epistle of the Apostles*, according to which the words of Jesus were interrupted by 'a clap of thunder, lightning and an earthquake'. 'The skies were rent and a brilliant cloud [or a chariot of clouds—the *Merkaba*] which took Him away. Then the voices of many angels could be heard rejoicing and giving praise. . . . And when Jesus reached the sky we could hear Him say "Return in peace".' Among the ancient Jews, the truth about the *Merkaba*, a celestial vehicle of the angels, was kept secret and revealed only to a small number of initiates. (Cf. *La Kabbale*, by H. Serouya, Editions Grasset.)

CHAPTER SIXTEEN

The Ascension

THIS 'ASCENSION' towards an invisible 'beyond' assumes a unique importance; it is connected with other similar departures, which our History has recorded.

The Bible and several apocryphal texts (the word apocryphal has no bad meaning, and means only 'kept secret' and applies to texts which have not been read in public) accept as truth the taking to heaven of Enoch, the descendant of Seth and the ancestor of Noah. In Ecclesiasticus xliv, 16 we read: 'Enoch pleased the Lord and was translated, being an example of repentance to all generations.'

Elijah, we have seen, underwent the same fate.

Other ascensions are of less importance as they only lasted a short time. Those who benefited from them after having experienced unforgettable contact with a distant reality declare themselves incapable of describing them owing to a lack of suitable vocabulary. The ascension of Isaiah the Pastor of Hermas gives us rather too much accurate detail for it to appear to us to be authentic. . . . Doubtless the accounts of these fortunate ones suffered a fate similar to the book of Ezekiel: written out from memory by the scribes, they were embellished with inappropriate ornament, in order to appeal to the imagination of their contemporaries.

The case of Saul of Tarsus, better known under the name

of St Paul, makes us think that certain human beings have had similar experiences, but did not think it necessary to proclaim them to the world. Thus it was only after fourteen years of silence that St Paul agreed to make public the experience which he had undergone, the day of his visit to the beyond; in addition he only did so when he was compelled to do so and used the third person singular as if a kind of bashfulness prevented him from admitting to such great glory. Writing of himself, he said (II Corinthians xii, 2–4):

'I knew a man in Christ above fourteen years ago (whether in the body, I cannot tell; or whether out of the body, I cannot tell: God knoweth); How that he was caught up into paradise, and heard such unspeakable words, which it is not lawful for a man to utter.'

It is a great pity that the apostle did not preserve a clearer memory of the occurrence, and that he did not know whether or not his body followed him in this adventure. Owing to this uncertainty we are inclined to think that his material covering remained safe and sound on the Earth while his soul experienced the delightful wonders of the ecstasy: the phenomenon, although unexplained, has been known to mystics of every age.

But it is equally probable that Paul was taken up in his body, as there are notable precedents for this, especially that which we know as the Ascension of Christ. According to the official Roman Catholic doctrine, Jesus went to Heaven not as a phantom but as a being which clearly had a body. 'Jesus went up to Heaven as a man, that is to say, body and soul, and different from the saints whose body remains in the tomb until the glorious resurrection.' (*La Doctrine Catholique*, by the Abbé Boulanger.)

This leads us to ask what became of this body and in what place it was going to live, since, according to St Thomas Aquinas (*Somme Théologique*, question 83, on the Subtlety of the Bodies of the Elect) every body has, presumably, a dimension and a position in space. Therefore, after

His Ascension and before His return, Jesus would have, in some manner, to be physically present in a place which it is impossible for us to define.

To assume that this place is a planet, a sun, or a constellation is to go far from what we have just said and we run the risk of ridicule owing to naïvety. This is the time to draw attention to certain contemporary theories, put forward by eminent physicists, about the existence of 'parallel' universes between which occasional exchanges are possible —unless any such contact cause an explosion. ... But even if such theories cannot be proved in ordinary language, they can be shown to be mathematically possible 'Unspeakable words, which it is not lawful for a man to hear,' as St Paul said. We will leave this problem to the specialists, who feel able to write, like M. Jacques Bergier:

'In separating the photon in the neutrino and the anti-neutrino at their arrival on one surface and putting them together when they leave it, one would succeed in creating the invisible man.' (*Les Murailles Invisibles*, Edition Del Duca.) Perhaps the glorious body of Jesus and several other privileged persons knew how to separate the photon. ... But there again we withdraw on account of our incompetence to discuss such things for fear we make some stupid error. After all, they are completely superfluous to the working out of our theory.

We have left to the last the Ascension of the body of Mary, the mother of Jesus, on account of its particular importance from the point of view that we are putting forth.

After the departure of her Son 'in the clouds', Mary was looked after by His friends, especially St John, who took her, it is said, to Ephesus, where she ended her days. There, when her time had come, she expired gently.

But when her disciples entered the room in order to carry away her body, there was no sign of Mary. The bed bore the marks of her body, but it was empty.

If we are not hindered by firmly established ideas regarding the irreversible character of death, according to the law of 'ancient nature', we can find a thousand reasons for believing that the Virgin Mary, at the present time, is still alive, owing to this mutation which was begun by her son. If we accept that Mary took on the new Yahvist nature, the incomprehensible facts of Lourdes and of Fatima, and of several other fortunate places can be explained by us relatively easily. . . .

It might be useful to point out here that it was on the occasion of the 'definition of the dogma of the Assumption of the Virgin', that a disc from outer space came and stood between the Sun and the attention of Pope Pius XII in 1950. We have told the story of this vision on pages 97–98, which links, rather strangely, the appearance of what were thought quite distinct phenomena, those of the Virgin Mary and those of flying saucers; something that is very difficult to get used to in the present state of our Earthly knowledge.

CHAPTER SEVENTEEN

The End of The World Has Not Taken Place

IT REMAINS to discuss the end of the world. . . .

But not the end of the world 'to come', a thing which it is fashionable to forecast from time to time, and which the menace of a nuclear war seems to promise will be in the near future. No, the end of the world which we wish to discuss is that which has not yet taken place.

The friends of Jesus of Nazareth lived and died quite convinced that the 'Day of the Lord', that is to say, the return of the Christ, the coming of the Messiah, the resurrection, the judgement, and finally, the accession of the elect to a new creation—would be very soon.

None of them, certainly, knew exactly when the date would be, nobody knew it ('no, not the angels in heaven, but my Father only', as Jesus said). In any case, the margin of doubt was no more than three decades. Indeed, the Nazarean himself had been explicit on this point:

'Verily I say unto you, This generation shall not pass till all these things be fulfilled', Jesus had declared (Matthew xxiv, 34). And in order to avoid the misleading interpretations which tried to replace the word 'generation' by the word 'race' Jesus added: 'Ye shall not have gone over the cities of Israel till the Son of Man be come' Matthew x, 23).

154

And Israel was quite a small country and it had not many large towns.

As for St Paul, he expressed the general view held by all the disciples very well when he wrote to the Thessalonians in the year A.D. 50:

'We which are alive and remain shall be caught up together with them in the clouds to meet the Lord in the air.' (I Thessalonians iv, 17). Everyone around him would share that assurance, which the following paragraphs do not deny: 'For yourselves know perfectly that the day of the Lord cometh as a thief in the night. For when they shall say Peace and safety; then sudden destruction cometh upon them, as travail upon a woman with child; and they shall not escape.' This stresses the unexpected of the day of judgement, and not that it would not come for many centuries. When Paul died, beheaded, he thought that he was only preceding his companions into the beyond by a short time. How would he suppose that this J-Day, which his master declared would be very soon, would be looked for indefinitely, century after century, until the phrase, 'we, the living, will still be there', did nothing more than raise a smile of cynicism?

What does this hesitation, this lost time, mean?

When a prophecy is not fulfilled it is something very serious, as it throws discredit on all the prophecies that accompany it. 'When a prophet speaketh in the name of the Lord, if the thing follow not, nor come to pass, that is the thing which the Lord has not spoken,' declares Deuteronomy xviii, 22.

Now as the announcement of a speedy return is repeated several times in the Gospel, the fact that it has not happened, and the long delay gave the believers of the time complete justification for turning from the Christian teachings; many indeed did this and treated the master and his disciples as false prophets.

What, they said, did not this 'seductor' faithfully promise that He would return, victorious and glorious, in a chariot of clouds? Would we not, at the same time, be changed into citizens of the kingdom that is not of this World? What has become of these promises, and who has seen in the sky, similar to a thunderbolt, the sign of the 'Son of Man'? Let us fear the preachers whose words are not fulfilled as that is proof that they are liars!...

We have to admit that this is all extremely embarrassing for the Christian; the Holy Fathers were the first to be worried by it. The commentators have in vain tried to explain away the difficulties; Jesus, they declared, was not really talking about the end of the world, but of the fall of Jerusalem (which took place in A.D. 70, that is about thirty-five years after his death); as for the Apostles, they were perhaps influenced by an 'infantile haste', impatient to see the most dear of their dreams realised; St Paul himself, when he wrote 'we which are alive and remain' meant something different from 'we which are alive', they spoke of those who would still be alive.... One can see the trouble which has been taken to find an evasion and a loop-hole. But the facts are there and it does no good to turn away from them and to conceal any uneasiness. It is best to face them.

First let us re-read the texts scattered through the four Gospels: we will see that they are precise. Here they are condensed and in a logical order.

'And as [Jesus] went out of the temple, one of his disciples saith unto him, Master, see what manner of stones and what buildings are here! And Jesus answering said unto him, Seest thou those great buildings? there shall not be left one stone upon another, that shall not be thrown down. And as he sat upon the mount of Olives over against the temple, Peter and James and John and Andrew asked him privately, Tell us, when shall these things be? and what shall be the sign when all these things shall be fulfilled?'

Jesus replied 'And as it was in the days of Noah so shall it be also in the days of the Son of Man. They did eat, they did drink, they married wives, they were given in marriage, until the day that Noah entered into the ark, and the flood came, and destroyed them all. Likewise also as it was in the days of Lot; they did eat, they drank, they bought, they sold, they planted, they builded; But the same day that Lot went out of Sodom it rained fire and brimstone and destroyed them all. Even thus shall it be in the day when the Son of Man is revealed.'

'And ye shall hear of wars and rumours of wars: see that ye be not troubled: for all these things must come to pass, but the end is not yet.'

'For they will deliver you up to the councils, and they will scourge you in their synagogues; and ye shall be brought before governors and kings for my sake for a testimony against them and the Gentiles. . . . But when they persecute you in this city, flee into another: for verily I say unto you, Ye shall not have gone over the cities of Israel until the Son of man be come.'

'And when ye shall see Jerusalem compassed with armies, then know that the desolation thereof is nigh. Then let them which are in Judea flee unto the mountains: and let them which are in the midst of it depart out; and let not them that are in the countries enter thereinto. For these be the days of vengeance, that all things are written may be fulfilled. But woe unto them that are with child and to them that give suck, in those days! for there shall be great distress in the land, and wrath upon this people. And they shall fall by the edge of the sword, and be led away captive into all nations: and Jerusalem shall be trodden down of the Gentiles until the times of the Gentiles be fulfilled.' (A prophecy which seems to be fulfilled by present history and the growth of Zionism, but the largest part of Jerusalem with the Holy places is in the hands of Jordan.)

'As for those things which ye behold, the days will come, in which there shall not be left one stone upon another that shall not be thrown down.' (A prophecy fulfilled in A.D. 70).

'When ye therefore shall see the abomination of desolation, spoken of by Daniel the prophet, stand in the holy place.'

'And they shall say unto you, See here or go there: go not after them nor follow them. For as the lightning that lighteneth out of the one part under heaven, shineth unto the other part under heaven; so shall also the Son of man be in his day.'

'For many shall come in my name, saying, I am Christ, and shall deceive many. . . . And then shall many be offended, and shall betray one another, and shall hate one another. And many false prophets shall arise and deceive many, And because iniquity shall abound the love of many shall wax cold. . . . Then if any man shall say unto you Lo, here is Christ, or there; believe it not. For there shall arise false Christs, and false prophets, and shall show great signs and wonders; insomuch that, if it were possible, they shall deceive the very elect. Behold I have told you before. . . .'

'So likewise ye, when ye see these things come to pass, know ye that the Kingdom of God is nigh at hand. Verily I say unto you, this generation shall not pass away till all be fulfilled.'

'Immediately after the tribulation of those days shall the sun be darkened and the moon shall not give her light, and the stars shall fall from heaven. . . .

'. . . and upon earth distress of nations, with perplexity; the sea and the waves roaring; Men's hearts failing them for fear, and for looking after those things which are coming to the earth: for the powers of heaven shall be shaken.'

'And then shall appear the sign of the Son of man in heaven: and then shall all the tribes of the Earth mourn, and they shall see the Son of man coming in the clouds of heaven with power and great glory. And he shall send his angels with a great sound of a trumpet, and they shall gather together his elect from the four winds and from one end of heaven to the other.'

'I tell you, in that night there shall be two men in one bed; the one shall be taken, and the other shall be left. Two

women shall be grinding together; the one shall be taken
and the other left.'

'The Son of Man shall send forth his angels, and they
shall gather out of his kingdom all things that offend, and
them which do iniquity; and shall cast them into a furnace
of fire: there shall be wailing and gnashing of teeth. Then
shall the righteous shine forth as the sun in the kingdom of
their Father.'

This account is made up from the following verses: Mark
xiii. 1-4; Luke xvii. 26-30; Matthew xxiv. 6; x. 17-18 and 23;
Luke xxi. 20-24 and 6; Matthew xxiv. 15; Luke xvii. 23-24;
Matthew xxiv. 5 and 10-12; xxiv. 23-25; Luke xxi. 31-32;
Matthew xxiv. 29; Luke xxi. 25-26; Matthew xxiv. 30-31;
Luke xvii. 34-35; and Matthew xiii. 41-43.

To this picture, St Paul goes on to add certain details
about the 'resurrection of the dead'; which he declared he
received from the lips of Jesus Himself, who was eternally
alive.

'Behold I show you a mystery; we shall not all sleep, but
we shall all be changed, In a moment, in the twinkling of an
eye, at the last trump: for the trumpet shall sound, and the
dead shall be raised incorruptible and we shall be changed.
For this corruptible must put on incorruption, and this
mortal must put on immortality.'

'But some men will say, How are the dead raised up?
and with what body do they come? Thou fool, that which
thou sowest, thou sowest not that body that shall be, but
bare grain, it may chance of other wheat, or of some other
grain. But God gave it a body as it hath pleased him, and
to every seed his own body, All flesh is not the same flesh:
but there is one kind of flesh of men, another flesh of
beasts, another of fishes, and another of birds. There are
also celestial bodies and bodies terrestrial: but the glory
of the celestial is one and the glory of the terrestrial is another. There is one glory of the sun, and another glory of
the moon, and another glory of the stars: for one star
differeth from another star in glory. So also is the resurrec-

tion of the dead. It is sown in corruption; it is raised in incorruption: It is sown in dishonour; it is raised in glory: it is sown in weakness; it is raised in power: it is sown in a normal Body; it is raised in a spiritual body, and there is a spiritual body.'

'For if we believe that Jesus died and rose again, even so them also which sleep in Jesus will God bring with him. For this we say unto you by the word of the Lord, that we which are alive and remain unto the coming of the Lord shall not prevent them which are asleep. For the Lord himself shall descend from heaven with a shout, with the voice of the archangel, and with the trump of God: and the dead in Christ shall rise first: Then we which are alive and remain shall be caught up together with them in the clouds, to meet the Lord in the air: and so shall we ever be with the Lord.'

This is made up of I Corinthians xv. 51-53 and 35-44 and I Thessalonians iv. 15-17.

This collection of texts gives us the outline of a drama in five acts:

    (1) Persecution of Christians;
    (2) Ruin of the Temple and destruction of Jerusalem;
    (3) Appearance of false Christs;
    (4) Cosmic catastrophes;
    (5) Landing of Yahvist forces with Jesus at their head...

Now, of these five acts, only the first two have taken place, after which the curtain falls for an interminable interval, which lasts for ever.

The end of the world has not taken place.

The Christian apologists seem to be prisoners of irreconcilable contradictions. Divine inspiration, according to the faith, guided the disciples and controlled their writings;

therefore they could not make any real mistake under that influence. But what they predicted did not happen. So if they did prophesy it, they were not inspired when they did so, or if they were inspired, they did not really make this prophecy.... The Biblical commentators chose sometimes one and sometimes the other explanation without daring to admit how unlikely they were.

There is, however, the possibility that a third solution exists.

This third solution is very real. It results from a reasoning that is so simple that one wonders why it was not thought of immediately; yet it seems that no one dared put it forth until now—perhaps too blind a piety only resulted in harming itself.

Let us look once again at the details of our problem:

Inspired men foretold an event which has not taken place. What does this prove? Quite simply that at the time when Jesus and His disciples predicted the speedy end of the world, they were giving an authentic revelation, in the sense that the downfall of the old world and the coming of the Kingdom of God was, *at that moment,* among the coming events of the Yahvist war, according to the plan drawn up in the beyond. If the kingdom did not come after the short interval expected, it was due to a modification in the plan itself.

Between the time that Christ preached the proximity of the Day of the Lord, and the time fixed for that day, there was a change of plan—a change which could be foreseen 'neither by the Son or the Angels in Heaven, but the Father alone.'

Thus everything has in fact happened as if, today, we were all reprieved.

Will we be accused once more of doing what we like with Holy Scripture, when we imagine that the divine plan, once it has been made, could be subject to modifications as it proceeded?

161

If one takes the trouble to refer to the Book of Jonah, one of the jewels of the Old Testament, one can find something there which vindicates what might otherwise be excessive audacity on our part. Jonah, this Hebrew poem tells us, was charged by God to announce to the inhabitants of Niniveh the Great that their sins would bring on, after a brief delay—forty days—the destruction of their city in the best tradition of Sodom and Gomorrha. Jonah tried in vain to avoid this thankless task. (Here the well-known episode of the whale takes place). Forced by events, he delivers the message to the men of Niniveh that he has been asked, although he did not wish to do so. But the people of Niniveh, frightened, gave up their wicked practises at once, and did penitence; their king gave them a lead by leaving his throne, clothing himself in a sack, and sitting in ashes to fast. Seeing this, God *modified His plan* and gave up the idea of destroying Niniveh the Great. The text tells of the anger of Jonah, who reproaches the Lord for making his prediction come to nothing and covering him with ridicule. But God, 'slow to anger and rich in grace', replied to him 'and should I not spare Niniveh, that great city, wherein are more than six score thousand persons that cannot discern between their right and their left hand and also much cattle?'

Thus the Bible, in the form of an apology, offers us well in advance a symbolic forecast of the first Christian ages. Christ Himself tried to establish a parallel between Himself and Jonah, (Cf. Luke xi. 30, 32): 'For as Jonas was a sign unto the Ninevites, so shall also the Son of Man be to this generation.... The men of Niniveh shall rise up in the judgement with this generation, and shall condemn it: for they repented at the preaching of Jonas; and behold a greater than Jonas is here.'

This is the text of St Luke, St Matthew (xii. 40) interprets the words of Christ differently and compares the sojourn of Jonah in the whale with the temporary death of Christ. The two versions are not incompatible, but complementary.

162

Finally, to succeed in refuting our critics, we hold other references in reserve. A New Testament text permits us to fix in the course of the year A.D. 51 the exact moment when a hesitation begins to appear in the execution of the plans of the beyond.

We have, let us say, benefited from a reprieve. And the word 'benefited' seems very fair to us. Whatever was the haste of Paul's companions, who saw themselves quickly rid of their 'bodies of death,' undergoing suffering from the ancient law, the delay in the fulfilment of the promises of Jesus is a great advantage for us.

In order to measure the fulness of this advantage, we must imagine what would have happened if the Yahvist plans had not been disturbed by an unexpected circumstance. Let us suppose, that the interval is past and the drama went on as originally planned by its author.

Once Palestine had been devastated in A.D. 70, the Christian world would have seen a collection of false prophets arise, the last effort of the cornered Luciferian forces. Then, after a succession of cataclysms which would have been inevitable as a result of the large number of cosmic forces launched one after another, the final landing of the Yahvist forces 'like a river of fire', would have divided Humanity in two: on the one hand, those which our fathers called 'the Elect', a small number—and on the other, the 'condemned' (the huge majority).

But already we are restive. Such a discrimination offends our modern sense of justice, equality, fraternity. But let us keep a cool head and think.

This would, we believe take a very poor view of our extra-terrestrials (who have always been declared by psychic people to be in advance of human beings), if we believed them to be capable of such infantile distinction as the 'good' on one side and the 'bad' on the other. It would need a very simple mentality to make such a division, and we know as

163

a result of modern psychiatric advances, that man is full of contradictory tendencies. Jesus has already told us that the tares and the good seed are so entangled in us that it is impossible to tear out the one without tearing out the other.

It is therefore probable that the last judgement will operate on other criteria. What therefore are the characteristics which make one man one of the elect, and another one of the condemned?

One can easily get an idea of this if one remembers that the earthly mission of the Son of Man did not consist entirely (as is far too often thought in our days) of spreading of moral discourses, for the greatest good of the nations. There were other things in His teachings besides morals. Jesus had come, in fact, to 'save what was lost', to repair what had deteriorated; and that by a mutation of species and the transmission of character acquired from an intellectual heritage (physically nourished in addition, by consecrated bread and wine, the 'flesh' and 'blood' of the first man of the new nature).

It can be understood that such a heritage could not be given out to anyone without adequate preparation. Our fellow-men have to be prepared for the change that is to come. 'And every man that striveth for mastery is temperate in all things. Now they do it to obtain a corruptible crown; but we are incorruptible.' (I Corinthians ix. 25). As well as moral doctrine, Jesus has given us advice similar to that of a doctor: do this, do not do that—not on account of some subjective ethics—but to obtain a cure.

Christ Himself said 'They that are whole need not a physician; but they that are sick. I came not to call the righteous, but sinners to repentance'. (Luke v. 31-32, Mark ii. 17).

There is no other way to interpret the standards of so dreadful a judgement: it is laid down quite clearly. Only those who subject themselves to an indispensible discipline will receive the new nature: whoever neglects to follow the advice of the doctor will not be 'cured'.

These, therefore, are the 'elect' who will inhabit the king-dom 'which is not of this world': the righteous, first, what-ever part of the world they come from, even if they never knew Jesus (who did not come to heal those who were well): that is those who follow the inclinations given by good ideas have led a life conforming to what was expected of them at the time: the Saints.

In all probability they would only form a small minority: as the instincts of the 'ancient nature' would weigh too heavily on the shoulders of our fellow-men for the righteous to be more than a very small minority.

After them would come therefore those among the sinners—Jew or pagan—who according to their trust in Jesus in a voluntary intellectual support have shown by acts of faith, hope, and love, their desire to have a share in the great inheritance. There would be more of these than the righteous, but still what a small minority when one thinks of all the people spread around the surface of the Earth, who have never heard of the code of the new nature preached!

What will happen to those people, the 'condemned', those driven back, unable to cross the frontier of deliverance?

Scripture, giving the Yahvist point of view, speaks of a negligible residue, the straw which is only good to be cast into the fire, the part that is unusable. An appalling waste the extent of which gives us nausea: a whole multitude which has never been touched on by Yahvism, the bar-barians of the north, the hordes in India and China, those of black Africa and the far-off isles. The unequivocal lan-guage of our fathers gives the idea of a condemnation, a reproach, we would say, rather, in our days, 'rejected be-cause of physical and mental inaptitude'.

'There, there is weeping and gnashing of teeth,' says the Gospel. Let us suppose, in fact, that the departure of the elect to the kingdom ('there will be a new heaven and a new earth') leave on our planet the men of the ancient nature in the state they were in before, that is to say, given temporary

165

joys, always subject to suffering and death, and with that, the lack of any hope for something better, but on the contrary, the certainty of a useless stagnation, henceforward deprived of any purpose. Would not this be a situation which would deserve the name of Hell?

Worse still: suppose that a cataclysm brought on conditions on Earth that made life unbearable for the 'condemned'. Suppose that mutation worked on them as well so that they, too, could not die and their body and soul would be for ever submitted to a trial that can neither be described or imagined?

Injustice? Disorder? Absurd extravagance of human potential? Bah! what anthropomorphic ideas! The history of the ancient nature, that of terrestrial evolution, gives many examples of similar waste; would not the establishment of a superior race, according to the Yahvist plan, be bought at a price like this?

The organisers from outer space do not usually trouble about expense when a cosmic interest is at stake. One could say that they would not hesitate to waste a whole lot of people to save a fortunate minority.... Let us remember the destruction of the dinosaurs and that of humanity before the flood; there is no reason that the establishment of a superior race, that of the mutated man, would be an exception; and if, by chance, the universal victory of the Yahvist forces would be so important would anything else be considered at all?

This seems to have been the case—at least until about the year A.D. 50.

At that time something happened, it seems, something that was not expected which slowed down the action of the Yahvist staff, and forced it gradually to give up its previous plans. Finally, the accomplishment of the prophecies, as in the case of Jonah, were apparently put off indefinitely.

Precisely between the year A.D. 50 and the year A.D. 51,

between the time when St Paul, having founded a church, that is to say a group of converts, at Thessalonika (present-day Salonika) wrote a first letter to the Christians in that town, in which he envisaged the return of Christ as 'imminent'—and that in which the same St Paul addressed to the same group the correction which follows:

'Now we beseech you, brethren, by the coming of our Lord Jesus Christ, and by our gathering together unto him, That ye be not shaken in mind, or be troubled, neither by spirit, nor by word, nor by letter as from us, as that the day of Christ is at hand. Let no man deceive you by any means: for that day shall not come, except there come a falling away first, and that man of sin shall be revealed, the son of perdition; Who opposeth and exalteth himself above all that is called God, or that is worshipped; so that he as God sitteth in the temple of God, showing himself that he is God. Remember ye not, that, when I was yet with you, I told you these things? And now ye know what withholdeth that he might be revealed in his time. For the mystery of iniquity doth already work: only he who now letteth will let, until he be taken out of the way. And then shall the Wicked be revealed, whom the Lord shall consume with the spirit of his mouth, and shall destroy with the brightness of his coming.'

These are mysterious words whose sense is hidden from us. If the Thessalonians knew what the apostle was writing about, if they knew the thing or the person which was holding up the appearance of the anti-Christ, we must admit that they have kept the secret very well.

In the French Jerusalem Bible, this passage (II Thessalonians ii. 1-8), is completed by the following note: 'Paul attributes the delay of the Parousia [or coming of Christ] to a reason which remains unknown to us, it is someone or something which held it back, a force or a person which prevented the manifestation of anti-Christ [which had to precede the Parousia]. On this subject Canon Osty remarked

167

that many hypotheses had been put forward, 'some of which were very extravagant'.

It is clear that the ancients 'knew' something which we know no longer; since the middle of the first century a force or a person came in the way of it, held it back, and stopped it. This opposition seemed then to be of short duration: but our history shows that by its continuity this obstacle was finally the master.

There has been no anti-Christ. There has been no end of the world, no judgement, no separation. There should never be any question of them except in our fevered minds when any specially great disaster makes us wonder if it be the prelude to something more.

What was this something? What was this someone? And for what reason did this force or this person cause to roll back indefinitely this terrible reckoning which would lead to the loss of most of us?

Here we are as if unravelling the mystery of a crime story, where a mysterious intercessor, rather than a criminal, has to be unmasked. Why do not we try to use common sense in this matter? It is not certain whether we shall succeed in solving this mystery, but it is worth trying. Will we not find something unexpected, something unlooked for, thanks to which our puzzle will be enriched by new detail, which is vitally important to understanding the whole problem?

It is reasonable to suppose that the giving up of a plan of this scale could not be put into force immediately the decision was made. We would find it difficult to imagine that the postponement of 'J-Day' (the 'Day of the Lord' in the Bible) would leave our species free to drift downstream to a destination of confusion and anarchy. Everything should be planned with the object of obtaining an exact result, while the menace of a sudden end continues to hang over our heads.

168

It would be interesting, in the light of what we have learned, to follow the progress of the Yahvist influence across the centuries that have gone by, and—that one makes no mistake about it—by 'Yahvist influence' we do not limit ourselves to the spreading of various religions whatever their particular form in which they have been officially clothed according to the countries and the peoples. It is easy to detect the mark of Yahvism even in the expression of views which claim to be anti-religious, as frequently happens in the case of atheistic socialism.

Compare, for example this text of Jean Jaurès: 'I have no fears about the religious future of humanity, of what is called the materialism of the socialists, or rather I rejoice, as religion cannot appear to men like something outside life, it must be part of life itself, understanding its closeness to it. . . . The true believers are those who wish to abolish the exploitation of man by man; also the hatreds between race and race, nation and nation, all the hatreds, and to create a true humanity which does not yet exist. But to create humanity is to create right, gentleness, love, and who knows that God is not at the bottom of all these things? . . . If I had the choice, I would choose the socialist workers. For I am sure that in my efforts to find absolute justice I would find God. . . . Even if the socialists at the moment are putting out all the stars in the sky, I would always march with them on the sombre road which leads to justice, a divine spark which is sufficient to light up all the Suns in all the depths of space.' (Extracts from a text published by Editions de Minuit, under the title of *La question religieuse et le socialisme*. Compare as well the *Express* of 7 January 1960).

If the spirit of non-violence, of mutual help, of justice and fraternity is still far from having established permanent harmony in human relations, one would have to have little faith if one could not admit that there have been improvements in that direction, even if we must limit ourselves to saying that these ideas, which are the aspiration of many

169

today, were formerly almost unknown to the masses. Undoubtedly there has been an evolution, humanity, by force of circumstances, draws closer and closer together, slowly acquires a sense of unity and its collective responsibility.

We must not let ourselves become unduly pessimistic by certain real but isolated facts, in any case it is not unlikely that twenty centuries of delay have allowed humanity to present itself to its judges in the beyond in very different conditions than itself existed a hundred years after the birth of Christ.

Naturally, the Luciferian forces have not been idle during that time and we do not have to look far to find traces of their activity, which they either hide or perform as sensational acts in broad daylight. The stake in the game is clothed with tragic gravity, in which we certainly have an interest, all of us, whoever we are, to have a clear conscience.

It is not less true that since this year A.D. 50, that humanity knew a reprieve which would allow him, if things continued to progress, even slowly, in the direction the Yahvists wanted to save almost everyone, instead of a small handful.

One can find an additional confirmation to everything that has been said in the variations which occur in the following texts:

(1) Matthew xxi. 19 'And when "Jesus" saw a fig tree in the way, he came to it, and found nothing thereon, but leaves only, and said unto it, Let no fruit grow on thee henceforward for ever. And presently the fig-tree withered away.'

(2) Luke xiii. 6-9 (written at the same time and after the ministry of St Paul): Jesus 'spake also this parable; A certain man had a fig tree planted in his vineyard; and he came and sought fruit thereon, but found none. Then said he to the dresser of his vineyard, Behold, these three years I come seeking fruit on this fig tree, and find none: cut it down, why cumbereth it the ground? And he answering said unto

him, Lord, let it alone this year also, till I shall dig about it and dung it: and if it bear fruit, well: and if not, then after that thou shalt cut it down.'

The intercession of the dresser of the vineyard, appealing for a delay appears in St Luke like an innovation which one looks for in vain in the earlier texts of St Matthew and St Mark.

However, we have seen just now that this care to preserve a great number is not like the usual tactics of the extra-terrestrials, who were more interested in the quality of the elect than their number, their point of view is based on cosmic necessity and not on the human point of view as are our views.

This is what will put us on the road to guess the exact identity of our intercessor. How could a human idea, completely and entirely human, become involved in the pre-occupation of the beyond so much as to oblige the Yahvist chiefs of staff to suspend their action, to adopt a different technique, another 'plan'?

We have looked among the scanty documents on this earth, thinking that they might give us this secret. The first idea which came to us was that it was the paraclete announced by Jesus (paraclete means counsel, defender), and identified later as the Holy Spirit. But the Holy Spirit is hardly a human intercessor, completely and entirely human.

On the other hand these terms can define a certain media-tress, human, entirely and only human, whose alliance with the Cherubim is revealed by the events of Fatima. Indeed, Fatima was the culmination of a series of events of the same type, of which the most famous was at Lourdes in 1858.

Twelve years before the appearances at Lourdes, on 19 September 1846, two children of the community of La Salette (Isère) had already undergone a similar experience, the first in time. They came back from the fields (where they were looking after the cows), declaring that they had

171

seen a large light at the bottom of a combe, coming from a sort of ball of fire. A 'beautiful lady', who was also radiating light, came up to them. Her feet did not touch the ground, neither did her body cast any shadow, even though the Sun was fairly high. This 'beautiful lady' who was not named, first pronounced the prophetic 'have no fear', according to the custom of friendly apparitions of the time; which was enough to remove any trace of fear among those to whom it was addressed. Then she began a very strange discourse (one of the things discussed was the potato harvest) in French at first, after which she repeated it in patois to be better understood. The beginning of this message is of particular interest to us, in the sense that it is an answer to the enigma of the great mediation:

'If my people do not wish to submit themselves, I shall be forced to let go the arm of my Son. It is so heavy that I can hold it no longer.' (The children said later that at these words that they believed that this Lady had a son who was striking her). 'Since the time that I suffered for you,' she continued 'You should pray well and do things well, but you can never repay me for the trouble I have undergone on behalf of you others. . . .'

A little further on she added:

'If the harvest is spoiled it is only your own fault.'

The children insisted that this Lady appeared overcome and shed real tears, which the intense luminosity of her face did not allow them to examine for long.

The vision of La Salette, the first of its kind, was hotly argued about in its day, and this can be understood. The personality of the two children did not present as many guarantees of honesty as that of Bernadette Soubirous at Lourdes or of Lucia at Fatima; the boy even went as far as retracting during a confession to the priest at Ars, saying that he had never seen the Holy Virgin, after which he pointed out that he meant that he was not sure at all if the 'beautiful Lady' was the Holy Virgin. . . . In short, we could give a hundred good reasons for disbelieving the tale until our attention was drawn to the fact that the words attributed to the Lady took on a very significant meaning when one put them in a context *which the shepherds of La Salette could have known nothing about beforehand.*

Furthermore, if the vision had been the only one of its kind, we would attach no value to it. But the 'miracle' of La Salette was the prelude to similar visions, whose authenticity is much more certain. One cannot even suspect these young countrymen to have copied their story from a previous event, as they were the first to tell how they had seen a 'Lady of Light' coming out of a 'globe of fire'.

The conversation of the Lady—at least the part we have quoted above—is very similar to the state of mind which could be that of Mary, a person completely human living an unknown life, and preoccupied even as far as tears with the well-being of her fellow human beings, and compromised by their malice and their thoughtlessness. 'I shall be forced to let go the arm of my Son,' that Son of whom she was to speak again at Fatima, nearly seventy years later, that 'He was not too shocked—do not shock Him too much.'

One fact whose character remains in doubt, when considered on its own, proves absolutely nothing. But when it is considered with other circumstances which complete it and form a coherent whole with it, and in a certain fashion, logical whole, it is no longer possible to reject it with a shrug of the shoulders.

CHAPTER EIGHTEEN

All Down The Ages

WHAT BECAME of our celestial visitors between the beginning of the Christian era and the middle of the nineteenth century? At first sight it might seem that there was little mention of those beings from other worlds during those seventeen hundred years.

But we do not want to leave our readers with a false impression of that kind. On the contrary, we have good reason to believe that relations 'between Heaven and Earth' (to use a convenient expression) did not slacken off at all during that particular period. History, of course, as we are normally taught it, does not draw our attention to any instances of intervention by beings from other worlds in the affairs of our countries. Our minds have become accustomed to describing as 'legendary' any event that does not appear to be directly explained by the natural laws as we know them at present, and is it not true to say that the work of the historian consists in separating reality from 'legend'? This being so, it is surely not surprising that accounts dealing with the activities of such visitors have gradually disappeared from our text-books, thereby giving the impression that hardly any accounts of that type exist.

It is true to say, 'hardly any', because our compilers of history, even those who are most firmly rooted in narrow positivist views, have not been able to omit altogether certain 'legends', without which it would appear that a link was missing from the logical sequence of events.

So not a single writer, no matter how objective he happens to be (and perhaps for the very reason that he *is* objective), would miss out the famous 'vision' when recounting the life of the emperor Constantine the Great. It took the form of a cross in the sky, accompanied by the words: *In hoc signo vinces,* i.e., by this sign you will conquer. One cannot but acknowledge that that 'legendary' occurrence played a decisive part in our history. There is no other explanation for the change of heart undergone by Constantine. Affected by that wonderful happening, he published the Edict of Milan in 313, in which he granted freedom of worship to all Christians in his territory, from Rome to Byzantium. There is no doubt that, if it had not been for that famous 'vision', the Western world would not look as it does today.

Similarly, the Arab world would have developed along very different lines if Mahomet had not received certain revelations from an 'angel' at the beginning of the seventh century. But very few people in the West would think of examining the 'fabulous' circumstances under which the Prophet became aware of his mission here on Earth. However, the small amount of information passed on to us by Islamic tradition is sufficient to give us food for thought. It shows us Mahomet withdrawing to Mount Hira and seeing a 'star' descend towards him. This is what the Koran says: 'By the star, when it descends, your brother is not dismayed. . . . It was at the highest horizon; then it descended and remained suspended. It was two bows' lengths away, or thereabout.' (Quoted in *Mahomet,* by Godefroy-Demombynes, edit. Albin Michel.) But after that first visit from the star the Prophet had to wait three years before it came again. In vain the desire to see Allah once more caused him to wander ceaselessly among the ravines of Mount Hira, until the day when in a 'true vision' he saw himself

175

surrounded by a great gleaming light the colour of the dawn and there, before him, was the emissary of Allah, Djibril (our own 'angel' Gabriel), who had come to teach him to 'recite' the word of God. (We know that when this was finally put in the Koran, according to the custom of the Arab peoples, a great number of analogies with the revelations of Judaism and Christianity and also some notable differences were found. We are inclined to attribute these analogies to the very real unity of the sources and the divergencies to interpretations made by men of very different temperaments.) We might add that Mahomet, like St Paul, was carried through the air from Mecca to Jerusalem first of all, and then to the 'highest heavens', and Islamic scholars have not been able to decide whether those journeys were undertaken 'in the spirit', or by 'body and soul' together, as is stated in certain texts.

Needless to say, Western commentators have only held to one single point in these accounts, namely, that Mahomet presented all the symptoms of epilepsy and frequently became a prey to hallucinations.

It would, however, be unfair to condemn our positivists, without acknowledging the fact that the Church of Rome in the Middle Ages engaged actively in suppressing certain rumours. Contrary to what one might have believed, it was the Church itself that barred most effectively any account dealing with beings or objects of extra-terrestrial origin, especially if those beings or objects were in danger of assuming any sort of material form in the eyes of believers.

Bishop Gregory of Tours in the sixth century described the mysterious passing of 'globes of fire' (in 583) in his *Histoire des Francs,* but in later years it became extremely dangerous to assert that one had had supernatural visions of any kind, and it was perhaps not always just from a sense of modesty that men who were in the truest sense holy tried to conceal for as long as possible from their fellows the favours that had been conferred on them. There was something ambiguous about the origin of these favours and it was not always easy to prove that they did not come from the Devil:

So it was not until the death of St Francis of Assisi that one of his companions, Brother Leon, was willing to tell how he had witnessed in September 1224 the descent of a 'ball of fire' upon Mount Alverno where the 'Poverello' had withdrawn in order to pray in solitude. And during that same night Brother Leon had found Francis in ecstasy, conversing aloud in the forest with an invisible person.... This is a story taken from Franciscan writings (*Troisième Considération, 1, Celano*) by Omer Englebert (*Vie de saint François d'Assisse*, édit. Albin Michel).

This same episode has recurred again and again down the ages, with as its leading character Moses or Elijah on Horeb, Mahomet on Mount Hira or Francis of Assisi on Alverno. As for the evidence of Brother Leon regarding the 'ball of fire' descending from the sky towards the summit of the mountain, it would not seem out of place at all among the accounts collected by modern flying saucer enthusiasts, and we have just as much or as little reason to believe it as to believe all these other reports.

It would be interesting to reopen the records of the great trials of the Middle Ages, some of which led to charges of witchcraft and others to canonisation. Even so it would be difficult to make a correct distinction between sincere accounts and distortions introduced not only by hysterical or terrorised witnesses, but by biased and dishonest clerks of court.

Will we ever know exactly what happened in the lonely fields beside Domrémy when Joan, or Jeanne la Lorraine, was feeding her sheep and suddenly saw a great light just before St Michael, the patron saint of knights, appeared— the archangel whose Jewish name means 'like God' and whom the fathers of old considered to be responsible for publishing the Law on Mount Sinai?

Joan herself was probably unaware of the glorious antecedents of the being who addressed her. But we, alas, know that that 'vision' brought Joan of Arc to the stake in 1431.

A century later, when the Reformation had brought about a decline in the authority of the Church of Rome in certain areas, there was a resurgence of spontaneous eye-witness accounts of strange celestial manifestations. In his book *Un Mythe Moderne,* Professor Carl Jung quotes two extracts from the Gazettes of Nuremberg and Basle, the gist of which is as follows (*Op. cit.,* pp. 223-224):

In Nuremberg on 14 April 1561 'many men and women' saw blood-red or bluish or black balls and 'circular discs' in large numbers in the neighbourhood of the rising sun. They also noticed two or three large 'pipes' (or cylindrical tubes) also containing balls (one thinks at once of mother-ships). In addition, the report mentions, amongst other things, luminous crosses. All these objects suddenly began to 'fight one another'. The spectacle lasted one hour, after which the whole carousel appeared to fall to the ground 'as if it was all on fire and everything was consumed amid a great haze.'

At Basle on 7 August 1566 at sunrise 'people saw a crowd of large black balls moving at great speed towards the sun, then they made a half-turn, colliding with one another as if they were fighting; a large number of them became red and fiery and thereafter they were consumed and their light went out.'

Professor Jung observes that 'the dark colour of the saucers (before it turned reddish) was probably due to the fact that they were seen against the light in relation to the rising sun.' He states also that these wonders were 'naturally' considered at the time as being warnings from Heaven.

During the same period Rome redoubled her vigilance and severity and imposed a systematic 'black-out' with regard to anything that might suggest or even hint at the existence of worlds beyond this world.

An Italian monk, Giordano Bruno, after quarrelling with his superiors and then with Calvin, published philosophical works where he asserted, among other things, that stellar space was infinite and was *peopled by innumerable creatures some of whom stood just as high above man as man himself did above the animals on Earth.* After this Bruno made the mistake of returning to Italy where he was at once arrested. He was convicted of heresy and granted a week in which to think things over and recant. He refused and was burnt at the stake in Rome in 1600.

From what did he derive that supreme assurance about extra-terrestrial beings that made him prefer death rather than recant? Perhaps we shall be able to guess.

The Renaissance witnessed the appearance of a whole bunch of literary works where various authors, in clear or in obscure language, told of their extraordinary adventures in which they were visited by terrifying creatures from other worlds who imparted secret knowledge to them. Who were these authors? Were they mad or joking?

Not at all. In most cases they were men renowned for their scientific minds and exalted ideas. They were mathematicians, historians, surgeons, physicians, astronomers. The report of their meetings with (real or imaginary) beings from other worlds is presented to the public in the form of memoirs, or as poems or impersonal stories, although they obviously contain autobiographical details. Among these writers we might mention the inspired Kepler, author of the famous 'laws', thanks to which Newton was later able to formulate his theories on universal gravity. Then there is Jerôme Cardan, well known for his contributions to algebra and chemistry and for inventing a mode of suspension that bears his name and was intended originally to isolate compasses from the movement of ships. Cardan gives as the

179

date when his visitors appeared the thirteenth day of August 1491, towards eight o'clock in the evening. He describes them as having the appearance of men dressed in doublets and red hose and we are inevitably reminded of the costume worn by Mephistopheles in the opera *Faust*.

We might mention at random the German Heidenberg, who was called Trithemius, and his fellow-countryman Agrippa de Nettesheim, the philosopher and cabbalist who was imprisoned for sorcery, and we must not forget Dante Alighieri or Dr Faust himself. . . . All of them, in one way or another, prided themselves on having been in touch with messengers from outer space and declared that they had received a part of their immense knowledge from them.

This strange device was thought to have been copied from a literary custom beloved by the men of old. Long before, Socrates and Pythagoras claimed to have received inspiration from *daemons* (a Greek term not translated adequately by 'demon', as it means rather, a non-human entity). During a period like the Renaissance, when Classical thinkers were very fashionable, it was natural that this example should be widely followed by poets and philosophers.

But one merely has to consult the facts to find out that the patronage of supranormal beings in the sixteenth and seventeenth centuries did not always benefit the recipients. They incurred considerable risks and were in danger of being imprisoned or put to death. So a certain amount of courage was needed on the part of those who dared to exercise these privileges. In the light of this, it is difficult to assert that this behaviour was merely a concession to some fleeting fashion.

But we must not go to the extreme of believing all those accounts because of the many divergencies evident in them. It is quite likely that these authors, whose history suggests that they were all at one time in touch with 'secret societies', such as the sect of the Rosicrucians, did indeed derive a part of their knowledge from obscure sources, out of reach of the ordinary man.

Several of these writings, among which one must include *l'Autre Monde,* published in the seventeenth century by Cyrano de Bergerac, the Gascon poet who inspired Rostand, describe 'imaginary journeys' to the Sun or the Moon. It is not always easy to make a distinction between the products of pure phantasy and true scientific ideas, most of them far in advance of what was officially known at the time.

For example, the circumstances surrounding these flights to other planets (which the writers obviously had not made themselves) are described in such a way that we find ourselves wondering if all these details are not the same as are to be found in the great space adventures of today, three centuries later.

'The initial shock, wrote Johannes Kepler in his *Somnium* (with reference to the shock of acceleration), is the worst moment, for the traveller finds himself shot forward as if there had been a gunpowder explosion. . . . So he has to be treated with opiates beforehand; his limbs have to be carefully protected so that they will not be torn off and the effect of the rebound permeates his whole body. . . . Once he has completed the first part of the journey, it becomes easier, because in the course of such a long journey the body doubtless escapes from the mathematical forces of the Earth and enters the sphere of influence of the Moon, with the result that her forces become dominant. At this point we release the travellers and leave them to their own resources . . . They propel themselves by their own strength, as the magnetic forces of the Earth and the Moon both exert a pull on the body and keep it suspended, so the effect is that there seems to be no pull at all. As a result, its mass will turn of its own accord towards the Moon.'

After quoting the above passage in his book *Les Somnambules* (Edit. Calmann-Lévy, pp. 398-399), Arthur Koestler remarks that, by a truly astonishing piece of intuition, Kepler postulated in that work the existence of non-

181

gravitational zones which preoccupy our science fiction enthusiasts of today to such an extent.

The same would apply to the learned studies of Cyrano de Bergerac, which came out about 1650. Our 'comic poet' was taken up to the Moon in a 'machine' *propelled by three rocket-stages,* each of which detached itself automatically from the complete unit and fell to the ground as the fuel became used up, until the astronaut, left to his own devices, carried on his ballistic flight without the help of any motor. Is not this exactly what occurs with the stages of the American Saturn missile?

We find many extremely bewildering things in this 'other world' revealed to us by Cyrano, in particular, *permanently burning lamps* shining like little suns, which stop giving light when the transparent membrane protecting them is broken. And what about that incredible description of a 'talking book', the appearance of which resembles, detail by detail, the transistor radios we have at the present time? 'On opening the box,' wrote our poet, who was a contemporary of Louis XIII, 'I found a metal affair very like our clocks, full of all kinds of little springs and machinery. It is indeed a book, but a wonderful book without pages or writing in it; in short, it is a book for which we do not need our eyes. We only need our ears. So when anyone wishes to read he tightens up a great number of the little nerves of the machine, *then he turns the needle to the chapter he wants to listen to* and, as he does so, all the different sounds come out as if from a human mouth or a musical instrument.' (Cf. *L'Autre Monde,* new edition issued by the 'Club des Libraires', or Booksellers' Club, p. 108.)

Cyrano adds: 'After I had given some thought to this wonderful device for making books, I was no longer surprised to see that the young men of that country knew more at the age of sixteen or eighteen years than the greybeards in our own country. They learn to read as soon as they can speak and are never without reading material. In their rooms, or on walks, or in the town, or on journeys they can have thirty or so books of that kind in their pockets or hanging round their waist and they merely have to tighten up a spring if they want to hear a chapter...; in this way you can have all the great men, alive or dead, around you, speaking to you *viva voce.*' It should be noted that Cyrano also mentions the existence of a second book which looked like 'a monstrous pearl split in two', but owing to a voluntary omission or a cut made in the original text he does not explain how this worked. Are we to conclude that this 'monstrous pearl' represented a television screen?

The light, playful style adopted by Cyrano de Bergerac, even if we look upon it as a subterfuge dictated by prudence, does not encourage us to take that author seriously at all when he recounts his conversations with people from another planet. But what is certain is that he had read works by scholars and philosophers who advertised in all seriousness the contacts they had had with other worlds. And it is almost certain that he had many connections with Rosicrucians to whom he explicitly makes reference when he states that the members of that society had received, through the agency of extra-terrestrial messengers, 'many aptitudes and natural secrets that made them pass for great magicians'.

We would stress that phrase which reveals to us what Cyrano believed. As he saw it, men referred to as 'magicians' or 'miracle workers' merely applied purely 'natural' laws not yet known to the majority of human beings. At one time the harnessing of electricity to light tombs (permanently burning lamps) was thought to be magic, but today it would merely be a simple use of a common industrial product. How many *natural* realities, still thought to be fantastic in our twentieth century, will cease to appear so as future discoveries are made? The existence of beings outside this Earth may well be one of these realities.

According to Cyrano's predecessors, these 'Messengers'

183

appeared on Earth in a great variety of different forms, ranging from 'heavenly voices' to, as we have seen, dramatic presentations such as we find in *Faust*. We must admit that we find this very difficult to believe although, at the point we have reached, everything is possible.... In fact, these envoys from other worlds might well have different origins and pursue different aims, possibly hostile to one another, in the war that would seem to divide 'the family on High'. In addition to certain evil activities, including those which are supposed to have brought about the downfall of Dr Faust (born in Kittlingen in 1480), there are others which could come within the scope of the 'Yahvist' or Christian plan. One recalls in this connection the famous 'Memorial' of Blaise Pascal, the manuscript which was found after his death, sewn into the lining of his doublet. It said:

'The year of grace 1654, Monday 23rd November, from about ten-thirty in the evening till about twelve-thirty. FIRE. The God of Abraham and of Isaac and of Jacob, *not of the philosophers and scholars* [our italics]: Certainty: Certainty: Feeling, Joy, Peace. The God of Jesus Christ, Deum meum et Deum vestrum.... etc.'

The reader is doubtless beginning to see that more detailed research could be undertaken into the part played on Earth by beings from other worlds during the Middle Ages and the Renaissance and in modern times, both in East and West. A detailed study of that kind would fill a book as thick as this one.

The impression that there has been a renewal of activity from the middle of the nineteenth century arises perhaps merely from the progress we have made in communications and world news. Charles Fort, who wrote his *Book of the Damned* in 1919, many years before flying saucers attracted public attention, quotes newspaper cuttings mentioning luminous discs and other curiosities of the kind as far back as 1833. From that time onwards similar reports have appeared periodically here and there. We have enumerated some of them on p. 24, taken from specialised works. Others are still being discovered in collections of old newspapers.

But it must be admitted that these phenomena do seem to have been passing through *a peak period* recently, with the miracle of Fatima and the various waves of unidentified objects moving over different spots on the globe in straight lines.

If there really is a close connection between these manifestations and the common destiny of humanity, we must not be surprised to find that our visitors are anxious and perturbed, for this is an age when mankind is being threatened once more with destruction, as in the days of the flood.

CHAPTER NINETEEN

Conclusion

WE SHALL now leave the reader to his own reflections, without, however, nurturing too many illusions about what we have achieved in this book. We know in the light of our own experience that there is something so unusual about our theory that people will find it very hard to believe. A man of the twentieth century has to make a tremendous effort before he is prepared to class 'angels' or fiery phenomena or ascensions to heaven and other beings or happenings commonly described as 'supranormal' with real, and thus *in a certain sense,* 'natural' phenomena, as they are subject to the laws, as yet unknown, of a particular aspect of nature. By conferring a more or less *material* form (but what, after all, is matter?) on events that have hitherto been looked upon as belonging to some transcendental category—unless they happened to be considered as being purely 'symbolical' or indeed 'mythological' in the pejorative sense of the term—we are deliberately going against the mental habits of our contemporaries.

The curious thing is that we shall be attacked both by Christians and non-Christians, although for different reasons.

The latter will no doubt show their disappointment when they see the slender evidence we have brought forward in support of our suggestions. But perhaps they are in too great a hurry. We are merely at the *theory* stage, and only now can we start looking round for proof, where such can be found. At the moment we are in the position of a man trying to reconstruct the facts by means of the methods customarily used in *historical criticism,* i.e., by studying the available *evidence.* And everyone is free to assess its credibility according to the criteria of probability, coherence and above all the extent to which a number of witnesses who are reputed to be trustworthy and unlikely to influence one another are able to produce accounts that tally.

We are quite well aware that the present age is particularly hostile to this type of method. All evidence has become open to suspicion as a matter of course because there have been too many fraudulent breaches of faith already. A man gives his word, but it is not believed any more in spite of all guarantees of honesty and sincerity. And yet the history of the peoples of the world which we studied at school and have no difficulty in believing is based on an examination of old accounts and men throughout the ages have been perfectly satisfied with them. Where could we search for *scientific* proof about the character of Cyrus the Great of Persia or exact details of the battle of Waterloo? We can only know about them from accounts passed on to us by *eye-witnesses.*

The same is true of the events described in the books of the Bible, which the positivists of the last century felt they could reject because they seemed improbable. In fact, many 'improbabilities' have been eliminated and doubts dispelled as a result of unexpected discoveries made recently by our scholars. From now onwards we must be circumspect and wary and not refute some happening out of hand merely because it seems fantastic.

It is, of course, possible that, as our knowledge grows, someone may come along to contradict all the suggestions outlined here and state firmly and categorically that they are wrong—and this will be a relief to many people! But it is equally possible that our theory may be confirmed in the not too distant future. One can well imagine the importance this would have. If it were suddenly established that in all probability worlds beyond this Earth had played a part in our historical evolution, all our old mental habits would be shaken to their foundations and overthrown, and this would be followed by quite unforeseeable repercussions in all fields of human activity—science, politics, economics, sociology and ethics.

And that it why, although definite *proof* is not available at the moment, we feel that events which have been neglected in the past should be brought to the notice of our contemporaries. We should study this far-reaching problem with the serious attention it deserves and delve more deeply into it.

Others among our readers will accuse us of allocating the lion's share to one particular religion and appearing to be biased. To these people we would say that it is not our fault if the identity found to exist between the terms used to describe flying saucers on the one hand and the 'dancing Sun' of Fatima on the other inevitably causes investigations to be pursued in one particular direction.

We would remind them of the words of Teilhard de Chardin. They were written in a very different context and yet they could apply here:

'As soon as knowledge passes the preliminary stage of analytical investigations and reaches synthesis—a synthesis culminating naturally in the realisation of a higher state of humanity—it finds itself led on to anticipate and speculate on the future and the totality of things. . . . When we turn towards this totality and the future we are also obliged to deal with religion.' (*Le Phénomène humain*, p. 317, edit. du Seuil.)

Looking at it from the opposite point of view, some Christians may feel shocked because we have endowed with a tangible and physical character realities which they had been in the habit of enclosing within the realms of pure and impenetrable transcendence. We must pause to deal with this. If that reproach is well founded it could be a serious matter.

It is unfortunately a fact that a superficial reader who has hurried through the book might gain the gloomy impression from what has gone before that he is living in a strangely narrow universe. Where, in the midst of it all, is the God of our fathers, the infinite being beyond all earthly knowledge and time itself? We would appear to have replaced Him by demi-gods, demi-urges imbued with a spirit of petty rivalry and busily keeping a war going. The victims of which are, incidentally, us poor mortals. That is not a very reassuring view of things. It will disappoint some people and arouse in others a feeling of rebellion. Have we not replaced the evocative glory and brilliance of the divine fire by metal space-ships, similar to craft that we might one day be able to build in our own factories? And, finally, although we have taken great care not to say anything that might give rise to an interpretation of that kind, some people will accuse us of having insinuated that the father of Jesus is not the first person in the Holy Trinity, but merely one of those cosmic beings referred to as 'archangels', of whom there appear to be countless numbers in this vast galaxy. . . .

We shall protest all the more violently against that accusation because, it must be admitted, appearances are against us.

It was in fact our intention in this book to confine ourselves to a comparison of *existing documents*, our rôle being merely to compile and collate. We would take care not to introduce *any philosophical interpretation of our own* into the text: metaphysical extrapolation had no place in an account that we were endeavouring to make *as objective as possible*. So we have systematically thrust aside anything

189

that might be looked on as being a matter of personal opinion or even as reflecting adherence to an official doctrine of any kind whatsoever. We did not set out to construct from evidence already known a new and original intellectual edifice for which its creator would alone be answerable.

But a few considered statements do appear to be unavoidable, even if only to counter the criticism that will undoubtedly be directed against us, especially with regard to the questions we have raised above. Let us briefly try to put things straight.

Firstly, we wonder how a cosmos peopled by thinking beings endowed with physical faculties superior to our own, and whose nature and thinking habits and plans are beyond us, should for that very reason dwindle into a narrow and restricted universe in our eyes.

Secondly, how could the discovery of these inhabitants, whose presence had previously gone unsuspected, impair in any way the infinite, all-powerful and transcendental attributes or the absolute goodness of the creator?

Let us first of all consider the initial question. If we men find it hard to accept the idea of being dominated by superior beings, it is because of our present lack of imagination and our pride as humanists. In our anthropocentrism we have long been in the habit of viewing human nature as the *nec plus ultra* of universal creation, and so even an open-minded man like Teilhard de Chardin, writing in 1945, considered man as 'the most advanced and so the most precious of all planetary elements' (*L'Avenir de l'Homme*, p. 143).

It was not long before Father Teilhard de Chardin abandoned that illusion. In a text that was probably written around 1954, i.e., a year before his death, he made the following amendment: 'We have every chance (indeed the certainty) of not finding ourselves, as we had thought, the only thinking particles drifting through the firmament. . . . *There must be* other inhabited worlds.' (*L'Apparition de*

190

l'Homme, La Place et la Répartition du Pensant dans l'Univers.)

Convinced of the universal superiority of man, those among us who are nevertheless prepared to contemplate the possible existence of a power and an intelligence capable of prevailing over those on Earth will in one stride cross the immensity of Creation and come directly to Him who has created all things, God and God alone. It would appear as if there were only one way of rising higher than human nature—by being God. In his self-conceit man is only willing to measure himself against the infinite, no doubt because he thinks that no one could be better than him without being absolutely perfect. Is it not wiser to visualise an infinite number of intermediate stages between our own poor human condition and absolute perfection, with an infinite number of living and thinking beings at all these stages?

And there is nothing to prevent us from visualising the presence of thinking beings who, although superior to man in some respects, are inferior to him according to other criteria. Tradition had it that man would in the future be called upon to *'judge angels'*. (Cf. St Paul, I Cor. vi. 3).

But here our own mental limitations come into play. When we say, 'living and thinking beings', most of us are unable to depart from our anthropomorphic prejudices which lead us on to imagine 'Martians', i.e., animal species comparable with our own. The practice of haphazardly issuing them with an odd number of limbs or even, as science fiction writers do, portraying them as vaguely gelatinous or gaseous 'substances' does not alter this at all. We always fall into the error of endowing them with human thoughts and feelings, such as the ambition to conquer or colonise, and we actually transfer to them opinions inspired by human criteria.

The British authority of astrophysics, Fred Hoyle, jokingly remarks in one of his books that most science fiction writers, in describing extra-terrestrial creatures, present them

191

as beings inspired with feelings of hostility towards man. This is quite an unfounded opinion, not supported by any objective findings; it merely expresses a very human tendency to project one's own faults on to someone else.

And when we jib at the idea that beings on a higher plane can, after their own fashion, be subject to dissensions and rivalries and antagonisms which remind us all too forcibly of our own conflicts, we are in danger of being told, as Job was in the Bible: (Job xxxviii)

'Who is this that darkeneth counsel by words without knowledge? ...
Where wast thou when I laid the foundations of the earth? declare, if thou hast understanding.
Who hath laid the measures thereof, if thou knowest? or who hath stretched the line upon it?
Whereupon are the foundations thereof fastened? or who laid the corner stone thereof;
When the morning stars sang together, and all the sons of God shouted for joy? ...
Wilt thou also disannul my judgement? wilt thou condemn me, that thou mayest be righteous?'

Let us admit, as did Job, that these are 'things too wonderful for us, which we know not.' But that certainly need not prevent us from trying to understand them and rise above ourselves, as our minds seek to penetrate with loving gentleness the vastness of the Infinite.

THE END